## PRAISE FOR
# MAIN CHARACTER ENERGY

"Main Character Energy is seriously SO GOOD. I feel like every chapter is written specifically about me. It's unreal how powerful it feels to truly feel seen. It's like I'm sitting in the room with Megan and she's talking directly to me. This is the book I've been waiting for!"

**— Shannon Krueger,** Brand Coach and Photographer

"MCE is the self-exploration and deep dive into finding your confidence and flourishing to live your most authentic self. Through Megan's exercises and journal prompts, you can start being the main character in your life immediately. As you read and start challenging yourself, it's like Megan is walking through it all with you from learning about her life story, too. MCE cuts to the core so the real growth can begin."

**— Kaitlin Morrell,** LPC, School Counselor

"Using the techniques outlined in Main Character Energy, I've been able to set and maintain boundaries, leave toxic relationships, communicate better, and most importantly, show up for myself with confidence. I'm both proud and relieved to see the way my life looks now because I've taken an active role in creating it."

**— Lyric Ellis,** Creating Confidence Society Member and Long-term Client

"Step into the spotlight of your own life with Main Character Energy as your guide! Megan's candid stories will make you laugh and cry as she shows you how to dismantle the "ick" that often stifles us. She arms you with an arsenal of tools to rewrite your story and embrace your authentic potential of your Main Character persona."

**— Ashlee Smith,** Human Ray of Sunshine

# MAIN CHARACTER ENERGY

## LESSONS ON HOW TO LEAD YOUR LIFE WITH AUTHENTICITY AND CONFIDENCE

**MEGAN REED**

For quantity sales or media inquiries, please contact the publisher at the website below.

*Printed and published in the United States of America.*

Megan Reed Coaching
**www.heymeganreed.com**

*Editing by* Sage Taylor Kingsley
*Photography by* Shannon Krueger
*Foreword by* Jenna Teague
*Cover Design by* Megan Reed
*Interior Layout by* Megan Reed

Paperback ISBN: 979-8-218-26619-6
Kindle eBook ASIN: B0CBN6MYB8

*For Sonora, my little Main Character.*
*May you always know and love who you truly are.*

# CONTENTS

# FOREWORD

The very first thing you'll learn about Megan as you start to read this book is how funny she is. Fully fucking hysterical, actually. That and how much she loves to cuss (as do I, apparently).

You'll also learn pretty quickly that for a large part of her life, funny was decidedly *not* what she wanted to be. *Nice* would have been preferable. You'll come to find out that "loving," "generous," and "selfless" were the exact descriptors she wished for when she dreamed about people toasting her at her future wedding.

Spoiler alert: Her wish never came true. But the wedding toast descriptors she actually received were so much better: Unapologetically authentic. True to herself.

Which brings me to the next thing you'll learn about Megan as you read this book: She doesn't care what other people think of her. In fact, she thinks how others see her is none of her business.

And before you say to yourself mid-eye roll, "Great, another magical unicorn IDGAF person telling me how easy it is to just live my truth without a care in the world," let me stop you right there.

*Insert record scratch*

Megan has been through *the shit* to get to where she is now. In fact, I had no idea of the full scope and magnitude of that shit until I read this book.

I had the great pleasure of getting to know Megan in January 2021 when she joined the Quantum Coaching Academy (QCA), a certification program for aspiring and established coaches that I helped create with the program's founder, Ashley Gordon.

As head mentor coach and co-facilitator in QCA, I had a front-row seat to Megan's personal and professional growth during that time, and, man, did she expand herself and her skills in massive ways. And even though I got to spend 100+ hours on live Zoom calls with her throughout her six months in the program, she shares powerful experiences in this book that I never even knew about at the time.

I also had the honor of becoming Megan's 1:1 coach in late 2021 through early 2022 as she was preparing for her upcoming maternity leave after the arrival of baby Sonora. It was during my time as her coach that I truly learned the depth and breadth of Megan's gifts. Graphic designer, photographer, branding genius, social media guru (*Have you seen her Reels?!?!*), writer, coach, entrepreneur, wife, mother, sister, daughter, gardener, chicken raiser... There's precious little this woman can't do.

And there's a reason for that.

Megan has lived through some hella perfectionism and people pleasing, so she knows firsthand what it's like to exist under the crushing expectation to do everything well (i.e. *perfectly*)—and keep a smile plastered on her face while doing it.

Relatable and inspiring? *Yes.*

Hysterical and wise? *Hell yes.*

The ideal blend of coach, mentor, and friend you want to hang out with all the time? *Check, check, and check.*

From page one, Megan shows you exactly who she is, and along the way, she helps you *discover exactly who you are* so you can claim the starring role in your life story. Through her personal anecdotes, coaching techniques, affirmations, journaling prompts, and reflection exercises, Megan brings clarity, depth, and a fuck ton of laughter to the process of embodying your Main Character Energy.

What are you waiting for?

*Cue your movie montage now...*

**JENNA TEAGUE**

*President and Director of Operations + Education for Quantum Coaching Academy, Co-Host of Middle Finger to Perfection Podcast*

# INTRODUCTION

Let me just set the scene for you, okay?

I'm sitting in my AirBnB loft above a glass-blowing shop in the middle of nowhere, Holton, Kansas, with a cup of microwaved Candy Cane Lane tea, spearmint essential oil diffusing, healing frequencies on my Bluetooth speaker, and Christmas decorations everywhere.

I left the big city for a weekend to escape to this quiet small town to work on my book.

Before I left, my husband said to me, "Make sure you don't fall in love with some blue-collar worker who hates Christmas, you know, since you're a business gal from the city."

*Holiday in Holton.*

Has a nice ring to it, doesn't it?

Catch it on the Netflix Top 10 next year.

To be clear, I have no intentions of falling in love with someone new. I'm here to write a book, after all. A book that's been on my heart something wild lately, and I'm so excited to have you here with me.

This book is about becoming the star of your own story. It's about me, my journey, and how I've been showing up in life with (or without) Main Character Energy.

It's about my path to authenticity and confidence...
And now, it's about **yours**.

"Main Character Energy" is the notion that we are all the main characters of our lives, and to really live as the main character, we must show up and share the fullest expression of ourselves.

No more dimming our light to make others comfortable.
No more apologizing for existing.
No more secondary-character shit.

*You are the main character.*

The main character of your own vlog, novel, documentary, movie, reality TV show, amateur porno—*show up however you prefer to show up.*

You are the star.

*But let's not confuse Main Character Energy with Big Dick Energy, okay?*

**Main Character Energy** = showing up as your true, authentic self, regardless of what anyone else says or thinks about you.

**Big Dick Energy** = walking around like you've got a giant wiener in your shorts and you want everyone to know about it.

Listen, no one cares about the size of your metaphorical penis. You're the star of your show either way.

In this book, I'll be diving into all the "fearless" (read: questionable, risky, out there, and/or dumb) things I've done and lessons I've learned along the way that you can apply to your life and business, if you have one.

And listen, you could literally just read the chapter titles of this book and go on your merry way, but you and I both know that's not the way our brains work, is it? You've seen these headings before. On your favorite motivational speaker's Instagram, hanging as wall art in your friend's apartment, and maybe even on a quirky little tea towel at your hip grandma's house.

These aren't new fucking ideas. As a matter of fact, there's no such thing as new ideas. There are only new ways of delivery, and new people who deliver them in their own unique ways.

So come along on this journey of definitely empowering, maybe educational, potentially emotional, and probably entertaining lessons. I'm going to be talking about myself a ton–I mean, duh, this book is literally called Main Character Energy and I just so happen to be the main character of my life–but as you feel yourself in these anecdotes and find the lessons resonating, I invite you to be curious with yourself.

Let whatever comes up, come up.

Lean into it.

No judgment.

This is a safe-ass space.

It is my hope, that through these chapters, you will find yourself relating and healing bits and pieces of yourself that maybe you didn't even know were there. The ol' skeletons in the closet coming out kinda thing—where you shine light on them and suddenly they're not so weird and creepy anymore.

I'm going to share some stories with you that I've never told anyone before, as well as journal entries I wrote in the thick of it to process my emotions.

And to be honest with you, I'm fucking terrified.

My stomach hurts just thinking about it.

I feel naked and exposed, yet excited at the same time.

How fucking magical to have the opportunity to shine a light on all of my shadows. For literally the entire world to see.

I'm tired of hiding.

Aren't you?

I'm going to share some deep shit.

While my general demeanor throughout this book will be a marriage of sarcastic millennial wit and authoritative sass mixed with creative inspiration, some of my stories will touch on sexual harrassment, depression, and suicide. I am not here to sugarcoat any of this.

I'm also going to share things I'm embarrassed about. *But that's the whole point, isn't it?*

What kind of main character doesn't have any flaws or quirks?

I've got a metric shit ton of them, actually. So buckle up, my friend, 'cuz you're in for a wild ride if you thought this book was gonna be me sharing about how cool and amazing and perfect I am.

I am cool and amazing, BTW.

Perfect? There's no such thing.

I'll also be sharing some affirmations, journal prompts, and exercises throughout the chapters. While you're a grown-ass human and you can do whatever you want, I highly encourage you to take a reading pause and do them.

Because self-awareness is the first piece of the puzzle when it comes to showing up as your true self. Seriously, how can you show up as yourself if you don't actually know who the fuck you are? So take the time for yourself.

Right here and right now.
Because when else will you?
Don't tell me you'll *"do it later."*

I think you've seen that film before, and the ending is the same every time, isn't it? *(Subtle T-Swift reference for my fans out there. Did you catch it?)*

The first time you read *Main Character Energy*, I recommend you read the chapters in order. Because while each chapter and lesson can stand on its own, I've curated a specific journey for you, and some chapters build off the ones before them.

The second time you read it, you have my permission to skip around to the lessons, affirmations, and journal prompts you need most in that moment.

In this book, I'm going to show you:
* How to step into your Main Character Energy.
* How to uncover what you actually want *(and go after it)*.
* How to show up as your most authentic self.
* How to love who you truly are.
* How to ditch the self-doubt and comparison.
* How to set boundaries and stand up for yourself.
* And how to unleash your most confident self.

But this isn't your regular how-to book, either.
There's no actual blueprint for this shit.

There's no *"follow these ten steps and you'll be the cool and confident main character for the rest of your life"* formula, so if you were looking for instant gratification and immediate results, I've got news for you:

Self-discovery is a journey.

It is a mountain with no summit. *(But the views as you climb are fucking spectacular!)*

Some days you're going to scale that mountain at lightning speed, while others you're just grateful the sun came up and your fire is still going.

You're here because you've decided to scale your mountain.

*You're here because you're ready for the next level.*

You're going to learn these lessons through my experiences, so if you're the type of person who loathes inspirational anecdotes and entertaining autobiographical shit, then this book is not for you. This is your permission slip to skip this book.

Don't come at me in the reviews saying, *"Zero stars. A waste of three hours, don't bother picking this book up because she talked about herself the entire time,"* Brenda, because I'm literally telling you right now that's what the next 297 pages look like for you.

I'm going to reference a higher power throughout this book—God, the Universe, Spirit, Mother Earth, Source, whatever you call your guiding light—and I invite you to insert whoever/whatever you recognize in its place if the term I use doesn't align.

As a casual disclaimer I feel obligated to provide for you, I'm going to be sharing some stories that might make shit weird for certain people involved, so for all intents and purposes, you can assume I've changed some of their names and that all references inferred and included are merely coincidental. Unless they aren't.

But you'll never know, will you?

*insert shit-eating grin here*

I also want to acknowledge that I am, indeed, an able-bodied white woman born in the United States. (I actually grew up believing that I was partially Native American, but it turns out my Nana lied and DNA tests have confirmed I am indeed 99.9% white.) I recognize this privilege, and know there are many of you out there who come from cultures, situations, and systems that have not been kind to you.

No matter your story, your environment has shaped and molded you into who you are today—and always—the main character of your life.

Oh yeah, another thing... If you're offended by curse words, I invite you to lean into that. How come? When did you decide to be offended by the modern English language? What meanings have you attached to these words? Whose voice is that in your head, really?

I will not be editing or "toning down" this book for you, so if this is something we disagree on, I totally understand if this is where we part ways. *(If you're even still here LOLLLL.)*

So without further ado, LFG, shall we?

# GO AFTER WHAT YOU WANT

If we haven't met, in real life, or on the Internet: Hey.

I'm Megan *(that's me on the cover in case you somehow missed it)*, and I'm a farm-raised Midwestern gal who loves black cats, Pink Drinks, crystals, and sriracha.

I don't eat gluten or dairy because #CrohnsDisease *(does the fact that I just hashtagged in a book make me old? I swear I know how hashtags work)*, and I'm deaf in my right ear.

At the time I'm writing this chapter, my husband of six years, Brandon, and I have a backyard garden with five chickens, a freezer full of homemade bone broth and venison, and a nine-month old baby girl named Sonora.

I share these details with you because I'm here to *personally* give you permission to do whatever the fuck you want in life, even if it doesn't make sense to anyone else when you put it all together.

*Catch me doing crunchy witchy shit AND going to Starbucks, you know what I mean?*

It only feels fitting to have one of the first chapters of my book be about going after what you want.

I want to write a book, so here the fuck I am. I feel like this is where I pause and let you know what to expect in this book. *Should I have included that in the introduction? Who the hell knows. We're including it here, because this is MY book and I get to do whatever I want.*

I'm going to be real and raw with you. I will not edit my thoughts or my words to be less—less offensive, less honest, or less "out there"—or this will turn into every other personal development book you've ever read.

If this is your first, welcome. You're in excellent hands.

The most important part of going after what you want is to first *identify* what that actually is. What do you truly desire? Is it more money? More energy? Travel? A hot tub? Time with your family? Inner peace? You want to be a stay-at-home-mom?

Tell me. But more importantly, tell yourself.

And don't tell me you desire to work a 9-5 job every day for the rest of your life if that's not what you truly want.

You must allow yourself to dream bigger.

Like, actually allow it.

I was on a strategy call with a productivity and burnout coach in 2020. She asked what my big goals were. I remember saying something like, "I want to have consistent $10k months."

Immediately she was like, "What else?"

*What do you mean, what else? That's the dream, isn't it?*

She said it sounded like I had never allowed myself to actually dream big.

And she was right.

Why?

Because I was afraid. What if I would never reach those goals? What would people say about my true desires? What if I was asking for too much? What if I tried and failed?

I wasn't allowing myself to dream big because it felt safer to play small.

If you never try, you'll never fail, right?

In my Midwest accent: *Ope.*

Listen: If you never acknowledge your dreams, there's a pretty good chance they'll never happen. How can God/The Universe/Whatever You Call Your Higher Power guide you if you won't be honest with yourself?

What is it that you truly want?

She was totally right; I'd never considered that. I remember exactly what I said back to her after taking a moment to think about it.

*I want to get paid to be myself.*

And that's still true. I also want to have my own Netflix comedy special. I want a tiny house in the woods and a condo in the city. I want to be massively compensated for my expertise.

If you don't already know about my business and what I do, I'm a certified Quantum Life and Success Coach who specializes in confidence and boundaries. *But you can just call me a Confidence Coach. It flows off the tongue way easier, and the alliteration is so sexy.*

3

I help people get out of their own way and ditch the self-doubt so they can discover the magic within themselves and go after what truly matters to them.

Or something like that.

*Raise your hand if your elevator pitch changes every 20 minutes.*

Okay, cool. Me too.

In general, my clients are business owners, entrepreneurs, and creative humans who know they were made for more and are tired of living their lives on autopilot. They're sick of people walking all over them, tired of over-committing to shit they don't even care about, and really just want to feel at peace and in control of their life.

And if you're here reading this, I have a pretty good feeling you might relate.

So, what is it?

What is that thing, that with more clarity and confidence, you'll be able to achieve?

What is it that you truly want?

What would you be able to accomplish if you had more self-confidence?

*Everything. That's what.*

Just imagine...

You could finally write that book.

You could quit your job and start that business.

You could find the love of your life.

You could get that raise.

You could land that promotion.

You could speak on stages to thousands of people.

You could love who you truly are.

You could show up on video on social media.

You could rock that bikini.

You could make a million dollars. *And then another.*

*Every single thing you want is 100% possible for you.*

If it's more time with your family, cool. If it's a billion dollars and a yacht off the Amalfi coast, also cool. This is your story, friend, and we're just living in it.

You must allow yourself the time and space to identify what you truly want. And right here and now I invite you to let go of the idea that there's one right answer to this, because this isn't a quiz. There are no wrong answers.

This is your story.

And what you want one day may not actually be the thing you want the next.

And that's fine.

Allow all of it.

Allow yourself to chase a dream that turns into a dead end.

Because I'll tell you one thing, confidence and clarity are built through action, and if you never dive into the pool, you will never learn you don't actually even like swimming because of the way the water burns your eyes and makes your ears pop if you go under too far.

You could buy a house tomorrow because it's your dream house and then move in and fucking hate it. I have a client in this exact situation, actually. It took them less than thirty days to decide it wasn't the house for their family; now they've found an even better house that checks all the boxes this one was missing.

But that would have never happened had they stayed in their original house.

**You must go after what you want to know what you want.**

A wild fucking concept, right? My brain hurts just looking at that sentence, and that's how you know it's good.

Essentially, if you never try, you'll never know.

And there's a difference between what you actually want and what you feel like you're *supposed* to want.

The American Dream and all that.

You "should" want a two-story house with a big yard and a white picket fence and a tall, handsome husband who works really hard for your family of four while you're at home cleaning and preparing the meals.

*Fuuuuuck that.*

If that's your dream, I fully support it. But it sure as shit ain't mine.

The American Dream is a dead idea that doesn't even begin to consider the nuances of the human experience.

If you want to be an influencer who gets paid to travel the world and share about gluten-free restaurants, fuck yeah.

You want to be a stay-at-home-mom and watch your kids grow up? Hell yes.

An activist for women's or animals' or LGBTQ+ rights?

A homesteader with a giant-ass garden?

A speaker on stages all over the world?

An author? A nurse? A coach? A photographer?

A tattoo artist? A European bikini waxer? A sous chef? An erotic poet?

Fuck. Yes.

Never let someone else's dream or the idea of what you *should* want hold you back from pursuing what truly lights you up.

Imagine what your life would look like if you consistently took action towards what you wanted, reflected on your progress, made the occasional pivot, and kept going, no matter what obstacles came your way.

For real, what would that look like for you?

You've only got one life, and time is your most precious resource, so if you spend your days doing shit you hate (or can barely tolerate) all day every day... it's not for you.

Because it's not WHO YOU ARE.

You're here, reading this book, because you know you were made for more.

You know you've got Main Character Energy, and you're ready to start showing up as your most authentic self, aren't you?

Right now, unless you're driving obviously *(why are you reading and driving?)*, get out a journal or a piece of paper and something to write with. We're diving in.

Set a 10-minute timer, and journal with these questions in mind:

What do you truly want?

If nothing could go wrong, and if money weren't an object, nobody would judge you, and you couldn't fail... What would you do?

What big dreams do you have in your heart?

What would be so fucking cool if you achieved?

Write it all out. Seriously, write it the fuck down. All of it.

Go big, and then go bigger.

Don't worry about the "how" right now. That's not what this exercise is about. We're big-picture dreaming, okay? Think about the 2020 Megan whose vague, nondescript dream was to make consistent $10k months when it turned out she desired *so much more* for her life.

When your ten minutes are up, I want you to look at your notes.

*What's on there that surprises you?*

*What's on there that excites you?*

If it's in your dreams, it's within your abilities.

Keep this somewhere visible and safe from pets and food-coated baby hands so you can read it as a reminder of the main character inside of you who's begging to come out and play.

## Go After What You Want Affirmation

*I am worthy of the very best in life, and I now lovingly allow myself to accept it.*

## Go After What You Want Exercise

1. Set a 10-minute timer and journal:

*a) What do you truly want?*

*b) If nothing could go wrong, money weren't an object, nobody would judge you, and you couldn't fail, what would you do?*

*c) What big dreams do you have in your heart?*

*d) What would be so fucking cool if you achieved?*

2. When your time is up, go back through your list and circle what excites you most.

3. Keep this somewhere safe, yet visible.

# OWN YOUR WEIRD

You know what feels good?
*Authenticity.*

It's YOU they came to see. You: all beautiful, weird, and relatable.

When you show up as your true, authentic self—that's when the magic happens.

That's when you attract your PEOPLE.

One of my biggest flexes is that I'm the same person on the Internet that I am in real life.

People still, to this day, ask my husband after seeing me on social media: *"Is she really like that in real life?"*

For real. He always laughs and says, "Yes, that's why I married her."

Because I'm authentically and confidently myself.

*I know who I am and I embrace her.*

Lately, I've had the pleasure of speaking at retreats and events for business owners and entrepreneurs (so I get to meet a lot of people in real life who follow me online) and for whatever reason, it pleasantly surprises people who meet me for the first time in person that I'm exactly who I say I am.

After just a few hours together, they'll say, "Megan, oh my God, I love you. You're exactly who I expected, only better." (Pretty much a direct quote.)

As someone who's been embodying my Main Character Energy for years, I fucking love this, *insert sunglasses emoji and big Leo vibes here* AND this baffles the shit outta me.

Why the fuck would I be someone else?

How exhausting must it be to pretend I'm anyone other than the person I truly am?

Actually, to be fair, I know firsthand how exhausting it is to pretend to be someone else.

I internally struggled with this for the first 25 years of my life, and it took a wedding and some deep self-reflection for me to realize that I had absolutely no idea who I was and who I wasn't.

Raise your hand if you're exhausted from showing up as a watered-down version of yourself because you:

a) don't know who you are,

b) feel like you're too much,

c) feel like you're not enough,

d) aren't confident in yourself, or

e) don't like who you've become.

I feel you.

I've been there.

You're SO not alone.

While this is far too common, it doesn't have to be your story anymore.

*It's time to own your weird.*

And don't tell me you aren't weird or don't desire to own your weird.

If you're not weird, you're lying.

If the idea of "owning your weird" strikes a chord that doesn't feel right, I want you to lean into that.

Let's investigate, okay?

When did you decide that "weird" was a bad thing?

For most children, "weird" is a word you never wanted to be called on the playground.

Being weird = being rejected.

So it's totally understandable that you'd shy away from that feeling, because no one wants to be rejected.

Let's reframe the word "weird," right here and right meow.

Weird is interesting.

Weird is character.

Weird is cool.

Weird is intellectual.

Weird is unique.

Weird is fun.

Weird is funny.

Weird is quirky.

Weird is real.

Weird is authentic.

Weird is creative.
Weird is magnetic.
Weird is IN.

Weird is the new polished.

When was the last time you met someone at a bar or event and loved how uptight, rehearsed, and regular they were?

We're not even close to halfway through the book and I know for a fact you know that's not Main Character Energy.

To be fair, I'm not hating on the people who have great posture, enjoy long walks on the beach, have a hypoaller-genic dog, and love their job in accounting.

Those are all great things.

But like... What else?

What makes you, YOU? Ya know? What are the things you're hiding from the world that make you who you truly are?

Sure, you like long walks on the beach, but what are you doing when you get home that the people of the world would find weird or interesting but you're hiding because you're afraid someone will judge you?

Every main character in a book or movie has quirks that make them more unique, relatable, and lovable. Your weirdness adds depth and zest.

So why hide it?

You don't want to be someone else.

What you WANT is to love who you already are.

To be confident and content in your own skin.

To find joy and meaning in your every day.
To make progress towards your dreams.

*Am I right?*

It's time to own your weird.

Because the more you own and love your weird, the more others love you for it.

Let's list it out. Grab your journal and write down ten things that you're proud of (or maybe not proud of but they're a big part of your story), or unpopular opinions you hold, or quirks that make you who you are.

A "Fun Facts about Weirdly Amazing Me" list, if you will. So the next time you're meeting a new group of people and they ask you to share a fun fact about yourself, good fucking news, you've got TEN fun facts and now you get to decide which one you want to tell them.

As for me:

1.    I can lick my elbow. And I'm like really fucking proud of it.

2.    I'm a trained storm spotter in Kansas.

3.    I once won a keg toss while on a ski trip in Steamboat Springs, CO.

4.    I'm deaf on my right side. I have congenital aural atresia, which basically means my ear canal just never opened.

5. I once attended an open casting call for *Playboy* and made it into the magazine. (*Ope, sorry, Mom and Dad.*)

6. I've been published in *Chicken Soup for the Soul*... twice!

7. My go-to karaoke songs are: "Baby Got Back" by Sir Mix-a-Lot and "Lose Yourself" by Eminem.

8. I've lost track of how many times I've shit myself. (Thanks, Crohn's and postpartum.)

9. I stand firm that celery is the worst fucking vegetable to walk this earth. It's like eating bitter basement water with dog hair in it.

10. I've seen my favorite musical, *Joseph and the Amazing Technicolor Dreamcoat*, more times than I can count on two hands.

Super fucking zesty, right?

Owning your weird is all about embracing the shit out of the unique aspects of your personality and individuality.

It means being proud of who you are and not trying to fit into society's dumb-ass mold.

A mold that says you should make yourself smaller/invisible and blend in and be polite and STFU and work hard and sacrifice your joy for others at all times.

You were not made to fit inside a box, my friend.

Owning your weird means embracing your quirks, your interests, and your passions, no matter how different they may seem from the norm. *This is Main Character Energy shit, remember?*

It means not being afraid to express yourself and be yourself, even if others don't understand or accept you.

I don't worry about what people might think, because *what other people think about me is none of my business.*

You know why? Because it's more a reflection of the other person than it is of me, and I/we can't control this. *And why are we trying?* Instead of worrying whether or not someone likes or approves of you, ask yourself: What do I like about myself?

Be like the dandelion in the spring—they bloom and thrive and spread their roots and they don't give a royal flying fuck what anyone thinks about it.

Someone being uncomfortable or judging you for being yourself is not a YOU problem.

In fact, it's a straight up THEM problem.

If something I do or say triggers something in someone, it's probably something they haven't processed or healed from.

Let me explain.

There was a woman at a big gym I used to frequent that always caught my attention when she was working out. She came in hot, singing and dancing around the machinery, smiling and lifting, and would move on to the next one just as fast as she arrived.

It triggered something in me.

Somehow, this woman I had never met, had managed to annoy the absolute fuck out of me, and I found myself judging her for being "too loud and obnoxious."

In reality, my judgments against her had absolutely nothing to do with her, and everything to do with me. She was bringing up feelings and reflecting shadows in parts of me that I either wasn't in love with or hadn't healed in myself.

I wanted her to dim her light to make me more comfortable.

*insert embarrassed emoji here*

When you find yourself judging someone, take a step back and reflect: What is this feeling trying to tell me?

Your thoughts are a mirror, reflecting your true desires.

I judged this woman because she felt free enough to be herself in public. She did not give one single fuck about existing and taking up space at the gym, whereas I felt small and embarrassed to be there around a bunch of other people "better than me."

The judgment I was holding against this woman was just my subconscious mind saying, "Hey, we see this, and we want it for ourselves, too."

I wanted to take up space.

I wanted to feel confident.

I wanted to have Main Character Energy.

I think about that woman and the lesson she taught me about myself a lot. *Thanks, confident gym lady. You're literally an inspiration.*

Another example of judgment being a mirror reflecting your true desires is when you're on vacation and you hear someone start commenting on people's bodies and the swimsuits they choose to wear.

"They should not be showing that much skin," they say, scrunching their nose up like it's absolutely disgusting and an outright shame for that person to be existing peacefully in their human body.

Or maybe, Brenda, you just wish you were more comfortable in yours?

**Someone judging you for being yourself is proof you're doing it right.**

Instead of trying to hide, dim, soften, or change what makes you different, it's time to embrace your weird and use it to your advantage.

You are you for a reason.

There was a time when I started my self-awareness journey when I didn't love the person I was and the qualities I was uncovering.

Like being funny, for example.

It actually bothered me for a really long time that people thought I was funny.

"Megan, you're so funny," I probably heard on a weekly basis.

Cool. I'm funny. Is that all?

Humor, for a long time for me, was a coping mechanism that I used to mask my depression.

So to be known as a funny person was, for me, a reminder that no one understood the pain I was in and how much I was hiding from the world to make others more comfortable.

When something made me uncomfortable, I'd make a joke.

Yet I didn't want to be known for being funny.

I wanted to be known for being kind. I wanted my friends at my wedding to give a speech about how they'd never met anyone so loving and generous and selfless as me.

But I was just funny.

I brought joy to their lives.

They could count on me for an honest opinion on what I thought about their outfit.

And that was it. I didn't love who I truly was, and I was lost because of it.

It sounds so stupid now.

I literally brought joy to people's lives around me and I was swirling in shame because it wasn't enough. It wasn't who I thought I wanted or needed to be to be worthy of love. I was doing everything I could to avoid leaning in to my unique and personal "weird" because it wasn't society's version of an outstanding citizen.

I spent so long fighting the humor because I wasn't willing to own my weird.

I was a watered-down version of myself.

As I began to lean in and unapologetically embrace myself for who I truly was, I began to release the need to hide myself.

"If there's anything I've learned from Megan [and Brandon], it's how to not care what other people think," our best man said in his wedding speech.

No, but here's the thing: I did care. I cared a fucking lot, actually.

But there came a point in my life where I decided I was done being a smaller version of myself. Little by little, I began honoring who I truly was and embracing my shadows. Shadows that sometimes made me feel like I was a little too much.

A little too blunt.

A little too honest.

A little too real.

A little over the line.

*It's who I am.*

I'm proud of who I am.

I remember the exact moment I believed this idea for the first time: *I'm proud of who I am.*

It was during a photoshoot where I was sitting for my friend's personal music project. The purpose of the shoot was to bring 3-5 songs that made you "feel something" so she could document the power music holds over the spectrum of human emotions.

Kesha's song, *Praying*, was playing in my headphones.

The moment she sang that line, "I'm proud of who I am," and it passed through my consciousness, a waterfall of hot tears came pouring out.

I released 25 years of pent-up anger, sadness, hurt, guilt, and shame.

I was done hiding.

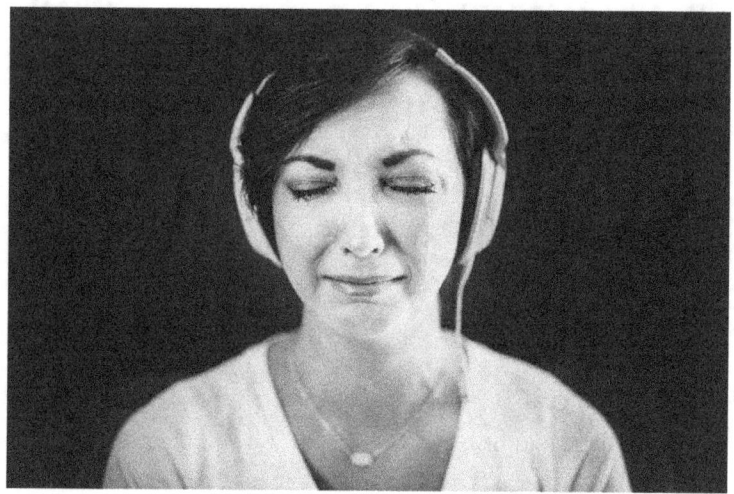

*photo credit: Sarah Nies Photography*

I knew who I'd been in the past, who I wanted to be in the present moment, and I was ready to love and accept myself—for all of it. For every single thing that had made me who I was.

Let me ask you something. Are you proud of who you are? Or is it time to let go of other people's opinions and start showing up as your authentic self?

It's time to be yourself.

To own your weird.

To be the same person in real life that you are on the Internet.

You are a unique and beautiful work of art, my friend, and it's time you start acting like it. Because these things you're hiding about yourself, weird or not, are your superpowers.

Tell me—what have you been hiding from the world that you're ready to let shine?

Are you actually really good at beatboxing, but you only do it in your car because you spit everywhere and your mom told you it was fucking gross?

Or maybe you've been battling robots in your basement, and it's time to start a community bot-battling league. *(Is that a thing? It's gotta be a thing.)*

Believe it or not, when you begin to embrace your weird, you begin to attract people like you who are also embracing their weird.

Like attracts like.

When you're showing up in the fullest expression of yourself, you're raising your energetic frequency and inviting others into your world who are also vibing high and experiencing life to the fullest.

I magnetically attract dream friends and clients into my energy because I'm showing up as my true authentic self in my life and coaching business.

I'm not calling people into my world who think I'm some-one else because they're going to be SEVERELY disappointed when they realize it was all a ruse and I'm not who they thought I was.

When you begin to truly OWN your weird, you start ques-tioning beliefs and releasing old stories you've been telling yourself that no longer serve you.

For example, I've ditched the belief that I need to wear business professional attire, have a full face of makeup, and watch my language to be seen as an expert in the field of personal development and business.

Because I definitely cuss.

I cuss, like, a lot.

And some people don't like that. And they're not afraid to tell me, either. Isn't it cool to have such a magical impact on another person's life that they feel called to let you know? *Hashtag blessed.*

Too bad you had to use the F word. Guess you're authentic!

16h   Like   Reply

U have alot to share! 🤍 🤍 Maybe I'm old but u could remove a few "fuck" and find a new descriptive word-one that "brands" u!!!

Sent from my iPhone

*^^Actual comments I got when I announced that I finished my first fucking draft, both within 24 hours of each other. I recom-mended they skip this book.*

I am not for these people, and that's okay, because I know I AM for a lot of others.

You are not for everyone, and not everyone is for you. And that's liberating AF, isn't it?

My clients fucking love that I cuss, because so do they.

It's refreshing for them to hear someone communicating just like they do—without the shame and bullshit pressure from society to constantly censor their words and "watch their mouth."

> It's one of my favorite things about you. Your dirty mouth. Because it's just as bad as mine.

> Hearing you say "fuck" in your content is therapeutic for me, so honestly fuck the haters 🖤

I've also ditched the belief that I need to have cool dreads and wear flowy yoga clothes to be seen as an intuitive healer.

I struggled with these beliefs for a long time, actually. The idea that I had to look a certain way to be real and for people to trust me.

But when I decided to lean into *my* story, and what *my* journey looked like, I was able to start doing whatever the fuck I wanted.

And it feels so good.

In fact, I'm gonna confidently show up on Instagram stories wearing the same outfit I had on yesterday because it was right next to the bed when I woke up because I know in my soul that the clothes I wear have nothing to do with the knowledge I have, the transformation I provide, and the human I am.

I choose to show up as myself.
I choose to own my weird.

*And I'm inviting you to do the same.*

## Own Your Weird Affirmation

*I graciously allow myself to be all of who I truly am.*

## Own Your Weird Exercises

1.  What are ten things that make you YOU? Write 'em out.

2.  Next time you notice yourself holding judgment against someone, take a beat and inquire within: *What is this mirror reflecting? What is this feeling trying to teach me about myself?*

# GET OUTTA YOUR OWN WAY

I can hear your inner critic now.

*"But Megan, what if I don't know who I am? What if I don't like who I am? What if other people don't like me?"*

Great questions, my friend. And I'm gonna answer them right back with more questions:

Whose voice is asking those questions?

Do you *really* not know who you are? Or have you just not given yourself the space to explore deeper into your own character development?

What cold-hard evidence do you have that other people don't like you? Do other people truly have beef with you? Or are you projecting and reflecting your own fears?

Raise your hand if you've heard these before:

*Who are you to achieve that?*

*You'll never stick to it, so why even try?*

*It didn't work before, so it won't work this time either.*

*Brenda is already doing it better than you are.*

*You should just give up now.*

That voice you're hearing belongs to your inner critic. Your ego. Your subconscious mind. Whatever you want to call the little bastard in your head whose prime directive is to "keep you safe" and protect you from any and all harm.

That voice in your head is YOURS.

And while it's doing a great job of keeping you safe, it's also been getting in your own way and keeping you stuck. *Good looking out, inner critic.*

Being "in your own way" comes from the idea that you are choosing to believe stories and repeat patterns that are holding you back and keep you spinning your wheels in the same place over and over again.

I'm talking about things like limiting beliefs, perfectionism, and procrastination. And the literal only person holding you back... is you.

*(I created a free eight-question quiz to help you uncover what it is that's secretly been holding you back: "Your Confidence Blindspot" as told by your favorite pop-culture characters. It's quick, fun, and insightful as fuck. Prepare to feel seen. You can take it here: heymeganreed.com/quiz.)*

Your inner critic is there to protect you from things like failure, rejection, and embarrassment— but it's also holding you back from success.

*What if instead of preparing for failure, you prepared for success?*

You've got big dreams and goals, and the voice in your head has you downplaying them all *just in case.* If you don't get your hopes up, it won't hurt so bad if it doesn't work out.

*Sounds familiar, doesn't it?*

Or if you don't get excited and tell anyone about potential new opportunities, no one will know if they don't come to fruition.

That little voice inside your head is doing its best to protect you.

But you know what's happening?

You're preparing to fail.

What would it look like if you prepared to succeed?

You'd show up differently, wouldn't you?

With confidence, courage, and zest.

Your subconscious mind is happy to believe in whatever you focus on, so why not focus on all the good shit?

Your progress.

Your accomplishments.

Your desires.

You are worthy of it all, but you're getting in your own way by listening to your inner critic.

Your inner critic is like the little guy "Fear" from the movie *Inside Out*, and Fear is afraid of change. (If you haven't seen it, HIGHLY recommend.)

Fear is afraid of leaving your comfort zone.

Fear is worried you'll get hurt or make a fool of yourself.

Fear wants you to stay the same, forever and ever, amen.

*But we're not here for that, are we?*

Next time you feel your inner critic stirring, acknowledge it, and say something like, "Thank you, inner critic, for protecting me. I am grateful to have you as a passenger in my car. As you can see, I'm the one in the driver's seat, so if you could cool it on the backseat driving, that'd be great. We've got dreams to chase, so buckle up, and shut your fucking mouth."

The more you notice and acknowledge your inner critic, the more you'll be able to move forward and make progress towards your goals without letting self-doubt hold you back.

It's like if you're climbing a mountain, and each day you look up at the summit and decide, that for whatever reason, you're not going to make it all the way to the top, so you give up, settle in, and remain cozy in your tent at camp.

Maybe you heard your brain say something that sounded completely logical.

*If you're not going to do it perfectly, what's the fucking point?*

*There's no way you're going to complete the task right now, so why even start?*

*You're just simply not worthy of accomplishing this.*

Your subconscious mind feeds your inner critic stories like this throughout the day, depending on what you're doing, in order to keep you "safe" from whatever new, dangerous, brave, or scary activity you're taking part in.

And you get to decide whether or not you believe 'em.

It's imperative to recognize and challenge these beliefs in order to break free from their constraints and step into your Main Character Energy.

Because you know your dreams were made for you, right?

You know wholeheartedly in your soul, with every fiber of your being, that these dreams are yours for a reason, and that you will accomplish them in your lifetime, don't you?

Your beliefs are one of the biggest limiting factors in your life right now.

I used to believe a lot of bullshit that held me back.

I used to believe that clarity, confidence, and motivation would just happen, but that kept me from building the life and business of my dreams.

*Turns out, clarity is built through aligned action.*

I used to believe other people's opinions of me mattered, but that kept me from living my life unapologetically. *It was freeing AF to let that shit go.*

I used to be embarrassed about not having my shit together, but that kept me from trying new things. *Let's just be real here. No one has their shit together. If you have your shit together, please call me.*

I used to be paralyzed by all the "what ifs," but that kept me from moving forward and evolving. *Try this on—what if you SUCCEED?*

I used to believe I had to be a carbon copy of everyone else to fit in, but that kept me from showing up authentically as my true self. *Turns out, people like the real me, too.*

I used to believe a lot of things, and you're in the same boat, too, aren't you?

These are all just our inner critic talking.

*What if I told you that one of the biggest predictors of your success was your belief in your abilities to achieve it?*

I see this with my clients all the time.

They procrastinate, listen to their inner critic, and delay their progress because their idea isn't "perfect" yet.

They put a new, incredible offer out into the world that they know is going to change lives, and because they don't believe it's going to "succeed," they don't talk about it because they don't want the world to know when it "fails," so then it ultimately does "fail" because they didn't talk about it in the first place.

*I've got thoughts on perfect, success, and failure. Don't worry, we'll dive in later.*

You wanna know what we uncover in our coaching sessions 92% of the time?

People are afraid of succeeding.

*Wait, what?*

Yeah, you read that right. Sure, failure would be scary.

But you know what else would be scary?

Achieving everything you've ever dreamed of.

*\*insert mind blown emoji here\**

The Universe will reflect your beliefs right back to you.

If you believe you're never going to make it, you're never going to make it.

If you believe no one will pay you big money for your expertise, no one will pay you big money for your expertise.

If you believe you have to say yes to everyone and everything to be worthy of love... you're going to end up saying yes to it all, aren't you?

At the root of the stories you're telling yourself, there's a common theme.

So what is it that's holding you back?

I see this with my clients a lot.

*Like, a lot a lot.*

Especially with creative entrepreneurs and business owners.

We'll be unpacking this on a call and I'll ask them something like: "How are those inner critic voices serving you?"

And they'll laugh, usually, and say, "They're not."

But the truth is, they ARE serving you.

Your inner critic is in your life as a protective mechanism.

The key is to dig into WHAT your inner critic is trying to protect you from.

What is the story you're telling yourself over and over again?

I remember the moment I uncovered the story my deepest inner critic was telling me.

It was in the middle of my Quantum Coaching certification program, where we were diving into the subconscious mind and how to coach clients through their limiting beliefs.

It was standard practice to lead each other through the exercises to: a) put in the work on ourselves so that we could heal and hold deeper space for our clients, b) experience the transformations for ourselves, and c) practice facilitating the tools.

After a guided meditation, we were given a list of words and phrases and instructed to circle the five that resonated most with us. *Peep the list below.*

| MY DEEPEST INNER CRITIC TELLS ME I AM... | | |
| --- | --- | --- |
| Lazy | Too sensitive | Greedy |
| Fearful | Not worthy | Unmotivated |
| Insecure | Not heard | Boring |
| Selfish | Confrontational | Not lovable |
| Not good enough | Uncaring | Not important |
| Not smart enough | Self-centered | Self doubting |
| Not special | Too aggressive | Victim |
| Manipulative | Always worrying | Not beautiful |

When we had completed that, the next step was to narrow it down to just three that resonated most. And after that, one.

When we had our root cause stories, we all counted down and said them out loud together.

"I'm not special," I said into a chaotic jumble of fifty other people speaking at once as I burst into tears.

It was hard to say out loud, but the release was unreal.

My entire life, I had been listening to the song of my inner critic on repeat. Everything I ever did was met with an underlying voice whispering that it wouldn't be good enough.

That I was unoriginal.

That there was nothing special about me.

How powerful would it be for you to uncover the story your deepest inner critic is telling you on repeat?

So powerful, right?

We got to name our inner critics, too.

Giving your inner critic a name can help you separate yourself from your thoughts and limiting beliefs.

The first name that came to mind was it. No second-guessing or overthinking it.

Mine is named Marlene, and she's a rough-and-tumble, hard-ass-bitch.

It's recommended you avoid naming your inner critic after someone in your life. I didn't know a Marlene at the time, but now I do, and it's always a good chuckle and a little awkward when I interact with her after the number of times I've cursed her name LOL.

My clients come up with the best names for their inner critics. We've got names like Regina George, Rebecca, Harry, Gertrude, Archibald—literally, you can name your inner critic whatever the hell you want. The whole point is to separate yourself from those negative thoughts and know that you are always free to choose a new and empowering thought.

*Marlene tells me I'm not special.*

For me to identify this about myself was a huge breakthrough.

The places I kept spinning my wheels and staying stuck made so much sense. The reasons I wasn't showing up more in my power was because my inner critic was telling me things like: "Who cares?" "You don't matter," and "There's nothing in this world that you could create that would be new or unique, so why are you even trying?"

That's what happened with this book.

For so many years, I longed to be an author, and yet my inner critic said, "Who the fuck do you think you are? What would you even write about? There's nothing special about you."

So I didn't write.

I can feel my inner critic right now, as I'm writing, too. Telling me this book won't be good enough, I'm not writing it fast enough, and that it's not going to add value to anyone's life.

Raise your hand if you've felt this way before.

*Yeah, I thought so.*

It's trying to keep me safe, and I get that.

But I AM SPECIAL, damn it! And I choose to *feel the fear and move forward anyway* because I know it's just my own inner critic getting in the way and nothing more.

Literally, you being here and reading this book right now is proof that our inner critics don't always have our best interests in mind.

In fact, our inner critic WANTS us to procrastinate, and we do it because it silences that little voice. It's the comfortable next step because with it, nothing has to change.

Not going after your dreams?

No problem!

If you never try, you'll never fail, am I right?

*Cool, Marlene. Fucking thanks.*

Imagine everything you could achieve if you had the confidence to make moves instead of listening to your inner critic and staying "stuck."

I'm challenging you *right now* to take a look at the things you've been procrastinating.

If they don't align, delegate 'em or delete 'em.

If they do align, get out of your own damn way and DO THEM.

Next time you catch yourself procrastinating on your big dreams, I want you to stop and ask yourself:

1. Is this just my inner critic getting in my way? (*If yes, move forward to the next question.*)
2. Is this dream truly in alignment? Do I really want it? (*If yes, move forward.*)
3. What story is my inner critic telling me?
4. What do I need to work through right now in order to release this and move forward?
5. What belief(s) can I embody to help silence my inner critic right now?

I believe that life gets to be fun. I believe that in order to confidently go after your dreams and embrace your Main Character Energy, you have *got* to get out of your own way.

You've gotta let go of the idea that it has to be hard. Or that you have to struggle. Or have this Come-to-Jesus moment or Near-Death Experience to be able to appreciate what you have or to live a happy and successful life.

Right here and right now, my friend, make the decision to get out of your own fucking way.

Identify your limiting beliefs and rewrite them.

Decide what you choose to believe.

Determine what is true for you.

You've got this.

## Get Outta Your Own Way Affirmation

*Whatever I choose to believe becomes true for me.*

## Get Outta Your Own Way Exercises

1. Referencing the list of things your deepest inner critic tells you, circle the top five that resonate the most. *From there, narrow it down to three, and then one. Write it down on a piece of paper, say it out loud, and then rip it up and throw it in the trash.*

2. Give your inner critic a name to help you separate yourself from the thoughts that are holding you back.

3. Next time you find yourself procrastinating, ask yourself:
   a) Is this just my inner critic getting in my way? *(If yes, move to the next question.)*
   b) Is this dream truly in alignment? Do I really want it? *(If yes, move forward.)*
   c) What story is my inner critic telling me?
   d) What do I need to work through right now in order to release this?
   e) What new, true, and empowering beliefs can I embody to help silence my inner critic right now?

# LEAVE YOUR COMFORT ZONE

You only live once, my friend. YOLO.

I remember when this saying started becoming a "thing" and we all said it ironically. *Am I allowed to say YOLO in a book, or is Drake's lawyer going to come knocking?*

Whatever, man.

YOLO.

*wipes anxious sweat from forehead*

You know what isn't easy?

Deciding between staying in your comfort zone (potentially limiting but cozy for a reason) versus healing, growing, and going after your dreams (scary as hell but SO rewarding).

Honestly, they're both viable options.

But lemme tell you—one of them will change your life, and one of them won't.

We just got done talking about getting out of your own way. Leaving your comfort zone is a big-ass piece of that pie.

Listen—it's called a comfort zone for a reason.

Cuz we're *cozy as fuck* there.

Your inner critic would fucking LOVE it if you would just stay in your safe and comfy little cocoon for the rest of your life. It would never have to work again.

But where's the fun in that? When's the last time you saw a movie where the main character didn't do anything new or exciting?

Leaving your comfort zone is the catalyst for all great things, because there is growth on the other side of that (temporary) discomfort.

Discomfort is good.
It means you're living.
Trying things.
Leveling up.
Putting yourself out there.

This fucking book is outside of my comfort zone.
It's testing literally every fiber of my being lately.

I'm on a lil' writing getaway right now with my biz bestie, Taylor, and we're both working on our books with the goal of completing our first drafts by the end of the trip.

It's 5 p.m. on Day Two and I've removed more words than I've added.

I just went outside in my socks and slippers with a big ol' glass of red wine to shout into the cold air, and instead, felt called to get on Instagram and story about being in my head and needing to take a break to reset.

Something I like to do is remind my audience that I'm still a human and struggle with the same shit they do. Keeping it real is one of my core values, and I'll never pretend I have it all together because that's fake news and ain't nobody got time for that "good vibes only" toxic positivity narrative.

Like yeah, I've done a shit ton of healing and know how to own my weird and embrace my Main Character Energy and show up as my authentic and confident self... but that doesn't mean I don't still run into my inner critic trying to slow me down as I level up.

New level, new devil.

Because you know what I've found through years of helping my clients build their confidence to achieve their wildest dreams?

When someone knows they were made for more and put on this Earth to make a difference in the lives of those around them, there's one pattern that keeps repeating: Their comfort zone is only comfortable for a little while.

*insert mind-blown emoji here*

As soon they reach their goals, they start itching for what's next. They long for growth. Challenge. Competition. Collaboration. They long to leave their comfort zone.

Because they know that their comfort zone is where dreams go to die.

*Did I just write that?*

I mean it. Your comfort zone can either be a graveyard of all of your best ideas, or it can be a place you're consistently leaving behind in pursuit of what's big in your heart. So ask yourself this next time you're hesitating between comfort and growth:

What would FUTURE YOU say to CURRENT YOU?

Discomfort is temporary. Discomfort looks like:

*Setting boundaries and saying no.*

*Trying something new.*

*Betting on yourself.*

*Healing unprocessed emotions.*

*Putting yourself out there.*

SO fucking uncomfortable, right?

Yet there's so much goodness to that short-term discomfort. Tell me:

a) What could your life look like a year from now if you took a leap today?

b) And what is it costing you to stay in your comfort zone?

I mean it. What would your life look like one year from now if you stayed cozy right where you are and made absolutely zero changes?

It could look like:

*Being overwhelmed and burnt out.*

*Having the same unfulfilling job you hate.*

*Still not really knowing who you are.*

*Lacking boundaries and feeling drained.*

*Spiraling in negative thoughts, guilt, and shame.*

Ope, right?

(Did you read that in my Midwestern accent? Cool, thanks.)

And, alternatively, what would your life look like if you simply made the decision to leave your comfort zone—even just a little bit—every single day for a year?

That's 365 days of progress.

If you did just thirty minutes of brave/scary/uncomfortable/new things every single day, that's 182 1/2 HOURS of progress per YEAR. (*Someone check my math. I was an art major for a reason.*)

I want you to imagine what's waiting for you on the other side of that many hours of intentionally leaving your comfort zone in pursuit of your dreams.

*You could host your own virtual stand up comedy show.*

*Attend an open mic night.*

*Perform in front of hundreds of people.*

*Have your own Netflix comedy special.*

(^^This is obviously my list. What's on yours?)

Now, I'm not saying you need to leave your comfort zone every day, but if you DID... you could do so much, couldn't you?

The things you want to do, the people you want to help, the business you want to build, the person you want to be... it all exists outside of your cozy little cocoon of mush.

Your mush cocoon. (Fuckin' gross.)

So when in doubt, choose yourself. You are an amazing and magical creature with so much more potential than you could ever even imagine.

The key is to continue pushing forward.

Choose growth.

Choose yourself.

Choose expansion.

Choose to level up.

Because you only live once.
So what's the point of playing it small?

We're all going to die.
And nothing matters.
And nobody cares.
And eventually no one will remember us.

How liberating is that?
*intentionally ignores the morbidity of previous statement*

Leaving your comfort zone can be scary as shit, but it can also lead to some of the most rewarding experiences in your life. When we stay within our lil' comfort zones, we're actively choosing to stay stuck and limit our personal, professional, creative, and spiritual growth.

Stepping outside of it can help you overcome your fears, develop badass skills, and gain that self-confidence you're looking for.

I can see your logical brain turning, "Yeah, but how do I actually do it, Megan?"

You want action steps. I get that.

And that's great because I fucking got 'em.

## How to Leave Your Comfort Zone
In five easy steps! *insert surprised emoji here*

1. **Identify your fears.** Understanding what's holding you back is the first step in overcoming your fear and leaving your comfort zone. *(You just did this in the last chapter. Neat.)*

2. **Start small.** Start with small, manageable steps and gradually increase the level of difficulty. I once heard Kathrin Zenkina, *(Manifestation Babe—we love her)*, on a podcast talking about the concept of "The Ladder of Believability" when it comes to manifestation, and I want you to apply it to leaving your comfort zone, too. As you do more things, each time, you'll be able to raise the level of discomfort a little bit. And you won't notice the shift compared to if you were to take a giant-ass leap all at once. Maybe you don't believe you could speak on a stage to millions of people right now, but could you speak on a stage to forty? Certainly feels less daunting, doesn't it?

3. **Surround yourself with positive influences.** Seek out people who will encourage and support you as you leave your comfort zone.

4. **Embrace failure as a lesson.** Making mistakes is a natural part of learning and should not be seen as failure. Embrace them as opportunities for growth and redirection.

5. **Believe in yourself.** You must have faith in your abilities and trust that you are capable of achieving your goals. *Because you 100% are.*

Next time you're feeling stagnant in your life or business, take a lil' inventory of what you've been up to recently.

If it's snuggling up on the couch and watching your favorite Netflix show with a glass of wine, that's totally cool. Maybe you're in a much-needed season of rest and recovery.

But if it's doom scrolling back and forth between Tik-Tok and Instagram and Facebook while drinking an entire bottle of wine and binge-watching the latest season of *Love is Blind*, there's a chance you're numbing to avoid something (and it's probably leaving your comfort zone to go after your dreams).

It's time to get off the couch, friend.

*Your life is waiting.*

## Leave Your Comfort Zone Affirmation

*I am becoming a better version of myself every day.*


## Leave Your Comfort Zone Exercises

1. Identify somewhere in your life or business you've been playing it safe.
   *a) What is it costing you to stay in your comfort zone?*
   *b) What's on the other side of this discomfort for you?*
   *c) What could your life look like a year from now if you made a commitment to your growth today?*

2. What do you need to work through right now in order to leave your comfort zone and move forward?

3. What resources can help you do this?

# CONFIDENCE STARTS WITH SELF-LOVE

*"You've always been so confident/fearless/motivated/upbeat/ other cool adjectives."*

I get this a lot, actually.

First of all, thanks. I know. *insert sunglasses emoji here*

Second of all, I'm not always. I'm afraid ALL THE FUCK-ING TIME. The only difference is, I don't let fear hold me back from the things that matter to me and light my soul on fire.

Third of all, you can do it too. The whole confidence thing, I mean.

You know how you create confidence?

1) You focus on self-discovery.

2) Then cultivate self-mastery.

3) While making time for self-love and expression.

When you focus on self-discovery, you're building your self-awareness muscle so you can identify and know things like your triggers, values, and what lights you up.

And subsequently you can begin to master things like your time, energy, and mind (the self-mastery piece) and then all of a sudden there's more room for joy, play, rest, and your creative passions (the self-expression piece). Which builds self-love, which builds confidence.

And the cycle continues.

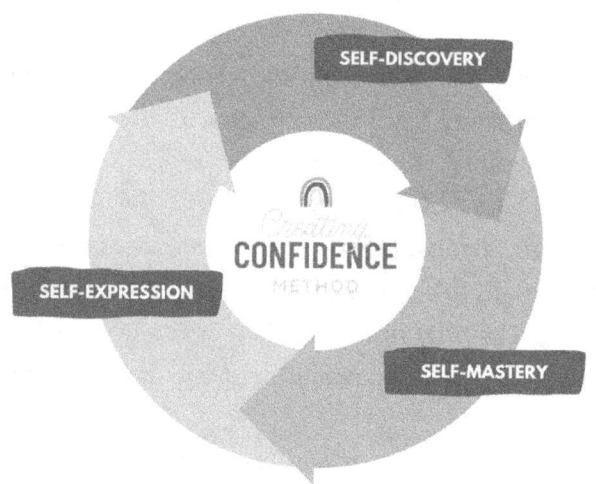

*The Creating Confidence® Method*

And there's WAY MORE where that came from, too.
A metric fuck ton's worth.

"But Megan," I hear you saying, "I'm already confident."
OR this classic: "I'm just not an outgoing kind of person."

Okay, great. Awesome. We love both of those.

There's this misconception that to be a confident person, you must also be extroverted and exude this obnoxious "look at me, I kick ass" energy all the time.

In reality, confidence is an inner knowing that you can fully trust and be yourself.

Confidence is quiet.

Confidence is loud.

Confidence is listening intently.

Confidence is speaking your truth.

Confidence is knowing you don't need to impress anyone.

Confidence is showing yourself—and others—what you're made of.

There isn't a one-size-fits-all, here's the step-by-step-instructions to cultivating confidence, since it can show up in so many different ways.

**Confidence can look like:**

Knowing who you are.

Having the courage to be your true authentic self.

Admitting when you need help.

Believing in yourself and your abilities.

Acknowledging your mistakes.

Healing your past wounds.

Pursuing your truth.

Expressing yourself through creativity.

Celebrating your wins.

Going after what really matters to you.

Setting boundaries and saying no.

Embracing your flaws.

Forgiving yourself and others.

Knowing when to quit.

Chasing your dreams unapologetically.

Each and every human on this Earth has their own version of what confidence looks and feels like. And damn, it's incredible when you're feeling it, isn't it?

Hot take alert: Confidence is not a skill that you learn.

*Ope—I said what I said.*

Confidence is not a skill that you learn; it's a state of being that you can access at any time.

Implying that confidence is a skill suggests that you're not innately born with it, when in reality, it's simply a state of mind. You've actually had the ability to leverage confidence since *before* you were even created.

I mean, think about it.

YOU'RE the winning sperm.

YOU made it inside the egg.

You fucking knew you were gonna, too.

You had absolutely no doubt.

The sperm that made you didn't have mad skills; it had confidence. *Dare I say, it had balls?*

Confidence is the way you act, the way you feel, the way you perceive things, and the stories you're telling yourself.

If you tell yourself, "I'm not confident," then you won't be.

You must identify as the kind of person who IS confident. Who EXUDES confidence from the inside out.

I know what you're thinking.
"So how come some people are better at it?"

You can be confident right now, simply by choosing to be.

There are certain situations where it may be more difficult to activate that confidence because of external forces, which is totally understandable.

And you could totally argue that "practice makes perfect," therefore confidence is a skill, but this isn't free-throw practice for your high school basketball team.

Confidence is the embodiment of a conscious trust in yourself.

The more you access and embody it, the quicker you'll activate it each and every time until eventually, this confidence is straight-up second nature.

Confident people are confident because they've figured out their secret sauce.
They know who they are.
They're owning their weird.
They've learned and are learning how to love themselves.

*Loving yourself for who you are is truly one of the biggest pieces of self-confidence.*

All too often I hear, "Megan, I don't even know where to start when it comes to confidence."

And I'm like, "Start with self-love." And that's the damn truth.

Practice loving and honoring yourself and you'll be building crucial neural pathways that will help you step into your most authentic and confident self without the self-doubt.

*That's the goal, right?*

While there's no single ultimate cake recipe for self-love—because not everyone's gonna vibe with the chocolate or the red velvet or the funfetti—there are some ingredients I recommend you have on hand so you can fuck around and find out which ingredients work best in your self-love cake.

## Self-Love and Confidence Cake

*Here are some simple ingredients you can begin to incorporate into your daily routine to help you cultivate an attitude and a lifestyle of self-love in order to create confidence—in no particular order:*

**One (1) cup: get the fuck outside.**
For the fresh air, grounding, sunshine, and that good ol' vitamin D.

**Two (2) cups: eat whole, nutrient-dense foods.**
Support your energy and immune system.

### Three (3) cups: make time for creativity.

Whether your cup of tea is art, dancing, gardening, or crocheting... just go play. Rest is productive, too, so recharge your brain and have some fun.

### Four (4) cups: move yo' body.

Whatever your favorite form of movement is, do it. Schedule it in, set reminders, get an accountability buddy or coach if you have to. Walking, running, weight-lifting, swimming, cycling, CrossFit, yoga, dancing, it doesn't matter. A body in motion stays in motion.

### Five (5) cups: practice mindfulness.

Check in with your mind and body daily. Breathe a deep belly breath. Journal. Meditate. Recite positive affirmations. Whatever the fuck brings you back to your awareness and mindfulness in this present moment.

### Six (6) cups: consume dark chocolate.

This one is happy science. Eat the cookie. Order the Chipotle. (Get the GUAC.) Yeah, you should fuel your body with nutritious foods, but you should also eat foods and drink beverages that bring you joy. It's a BOTH kind of situation, ya know? This is a recipe for self-love CAKE after all.

### Seven (7) cups: set boundaries.

You want more time for yourself? Start by saying no to more things. When you say yes to things you don't want to do or that don't align with your goals, you're taking time and energy away from things that actually matter. Your no empowers your yes.

**Eight (8) cups: read personal development books.**

Or any book, really. You're on a roll right now with this one. You're welcome. (You can also watch videos or listen to podcasts—however you best like to consume personal development content.)

The good news is you don't have to mix all these ingredients in at once (or ever). Your cake can be as simple or as fancy as you want, because it's yours and yours alone. No one else will be eating your cake, because it's is a fucking metaphor, so there's no wrong way to flavor it, bake it, or frost it.

Start small, and work on identifying as the type of person who loves themselves enough to *try.*

A barrier I see a lot is that people don't even know where to start, because for so long they've been focused on everyone else and to bring the spotlight back to themselves feels uncomfortable and weird.

That's why we're starting small, remember?
We're not trying to climb Mount Everest in a day.
First we've just got to get off the couch.

*Here are three little ways you can instantly shift your mood, raise your vibe, and create confidence through a self-love practice:*

**1) Put on your favorite outfit.**

Seriously, take off those sweats you've been wearing for the past few weeks and slide into something that makes you feel like your best self. My favorite outfits: Overalls, rompers, and jumpsuits. I've said it before and I'll say it a million times, but the harder to pee in, the better the outfit.

### 2) Get out of the house.

Go for a quick walk. Have lunch outside. Do a driveway workout. Take a deep breath of fresh air. Do lawn yoga or tai chi. Grab the mail. Walk your doggos around the block. Work in your garden. Read or have a cuppa something on your patio. If you need a reset, the great outdoors are ready to help.

### 3) Dance and sing to your favorite song.

I mean, like really fucking do it. Turn it up loud, and for three to five minutes or however long your jam is, GROOVE. Turn all the lights off if you need to or dance your ass off in front of a mirror and send sexy smiles to your gorgeous self. However you do it, just feel the energy and joy move through your body.

It's not the big, monumental moves we make that create confidence and change the way we feel about everything.

No. It's the small, daily efforts that encourage growth and allow us to scale our mountains with commitment, grace, self-trust, and beautiful, messy progress over time.

When it boils down to it, that's all that confidence really is, isn't it?

A deep trust in yourself, an inner knowing that you've got your own back, and a sense of peace because you can count on yourself to pull through and do the damn thing.

*Confidence is unconditional love and gratitude for the main character you are becoming.*

Remember, my friend: YOU are the winning sperm.

*It's time to act like it.*

## Confidence Starts with Self-Love Affirmation

*I love and accept myself fully, deeply, and unconditionally.*

## Confidence Starts with Self-Love Exercise

Identify which ingredients make up your ideal self-love and confidence cake, so the next time you're in need of a little TLC, you've got an action plan in place. *What ingredients could you add or substitute that would make your cake uniquely perfect and specifically baked just for you? How can you remind yourself to eat your cake?*

# FUCK PERFECTION

*Feck Perfuction.*

I saw this book on a shelf during a networking coffee date once, and it made me laugh.

The intentional spelling error basically shouted its existence at me.

How many times have you gotten in your own damn way by letting your perfectionistic tendencies take over control?

Perfectionism is another one of those things, like confidence, that looks different on everyone.

I'm an Enneagram One, a Leo, a graphic designer by trade, a chronic skin-picker, and my attention to detail is hyperactive, so it's safe to say that perfectionism runs real deep.

I like to say I'm a recovering perfectionist though, because I'm AWARE of my struggles and am actively working on letting go of my self-induced pressure of extreme excellence.

Awareness is key.

For me, perfectionism shows up through validation.

I work hard and do a good job and create beautiful things because words of affirmation is my love language, and I know that if I "get it right," someone might validate me.

*Sound familiar?*

This is a dangerous mind game for me to play *(and I fucking know it, too)* because if I don't receive the validation I was looking for, I can very quickly spiral into a negative thought shitstorm. *I'm not good enough. No one likes me. Why am I even doing this? What's the point?*

I find myself wanting to give up and start completely over, or worse—pour gasoline on everything, light a match, and burn it all to the ground.

*Oof, right?*

Perfectionism is a real time-wasting bitch.

You can find me on the weekends rewriting my to-do list because the first one didn't look good enough. *insert monkey covering eyes emoji here*

It's truly obnoxious.

One time I tried to hire a virtual assistant to help with some social media posts and when she delivered the files I then sent her a 15-minute video telling her everything I would've done differently.

I'm cringing just thinking about it.

If you've ever struggled with perfectionism, you know firsthand how draining it can be. Tell me, do any of these sound like you?

- You struggle to start projects.
- You struggle to complete projects.
- You have unrealistically high expectations.
- You hold yourself to the highest standards.
- You expect excellence from yourself and others.
- You're frequently disappointed when things don't go as planned.
- You can't delegate because nobody does it right and then you end up spending more time correcting them than if you did it yourself.
- You're exceptionally hard on yourself.
- No matter what you do, it's never quite good enough.

*Friend... I am right there with ya.*

I once spent 2.5 hours on an Instagram reel because I couldn't get the text to hit just right with the music.

Another time, in Nashville I had a photoshoot coming up and was getting my nails done by a beauty-school student who was about to graduate.

She needed credits, and I needed my nails done.

Cool, cool.

Perfect.

And it's taking for fucking everrrr, right?

Like an excruciatingly long time to where you could have flown to Kansas City, got your nails done there, and been back before she was finished.

She's on coat number two, and they look absolutely horrendous.

You know what I'm talking about, don't you?

There's bubbles in your pinky nail, the polish doesn't go to the edges on either thumb, there's junk all over your skin, and she smudged her own work on nails 2, 3, and 4.

Your skin is crawling, your neck is hot, and you can feel the silent rage bubbling under the surface about how much time you're wasting, the fact that your shaky, half-blind grandma could have done a better job, and wondering when you're going to have time to get your nails redone somewhere across town.

At the two-hour mark she goes, "Sorry this is taking a little longer than expected. I'm a perfectionist."

I was speechless.

You can't make this shit up.

My mouth would have dropped to the floor had I not been anxiously chewing on the inside of my cheek.

Perfectionism looks so different to everyone who is experiencing and identifying with it that for her, taking two hours to do a manicure meant she was doing a good job.

In retrospect, I like giving her the benefit of the doubt that there was likely a belief underlying there—a story she was telling herself—that in order to make it a valuable experience for me, she had to put in a solid amount of time and effort.

*"I have to work hard to make money. If it doesn't take me a long time, I didn't work hard enough, and I don't deserve to get paid the full amount."*

I hear this story in coaching sessions a lot.

The idea that if it's not perfect, you're not worthy.

And nothing is ever perfect, right?

So you're stuck in a shame cycle of feeling like a shitty human being/business owner who doesn't know much about anything and can't charge a certain rate because your work isn't good enough and maybe that means *you're not good enough.*

Or maybe she KNEW she wasn't very good at painting nails so she overcompensated, thinking that perhaps if she just spent a little longer on them I'd be less likely to complain to her supervisor or tell my friends about the rush job I got at the beauty school.

But here's the thing: she was fucking doing it anyway. And that's the magic of it.

She, the self-proclaimed perfectionist, wasn't letting her perfectionism stop her from showing up and practicing her craft.

One of the toxic-waste byproducts of perfectionism shows up as wheel spinning and feet dragging and "feeling stuck" because you're worried that if you can't do it right, you shouldn't do it at all.

If you can't be perfect, there's no point trying.

*Fuck that, right?*

Here's what I know about perfectionism: It's stupid.

It's your inner critic finding a way to let you know that you are, in fact, not enough.
Not good enough.
Not smart enough.
Not motivated enough.
Never have been.
Never will be.

She could have waited to go to beauty school until she was more "ready" but she was showing up and doing it anyway.

I see this with people at the gym, too. They think they have to exercise in private for months so that when they start showing up to the group workout class they're in better shape and they don't embarrass themselves.

> **"People are not afraid to start their dreams. They're just embarrassed to be seen starting small."**
>
> *~ Brendon Burchard*

Read that again.
*Seriously, go back and do it.*

The fact that she was willing to show up and start small is badass.

She didn't wait around for the perfect time to get started, because let's be honest. The perfect time to get started? The perfect time to go after your dreams?

There isn't one.

There is no such thing as the perfect time to do ANY-THING.

If there was, we'd all have found it by now.

There will always be something/someone stealing your time. So what's it gonna take for you to take charge of your life? To decide you're worth it and start showing up for yourself? To allow yourself to dream big and go after your goals?

Perfectionism is procrastination. Perfectionism invites you to do one of two things:

1. It invites you to simply wait and do nothing at all with the idea that no action is better than incorrect action. In reality, clarity is found through that intentional action. You must allow yourself to make mistakes, show up and suck at something, and fuck around and find shit out. If you never try, you will literally never know. *Speaking of mistakes, there's no such thing. There are only lessons and learning opportunities.*

2. It invites you to work and rework and revise and pivot and overanalyze and beat a dead horse to the point that you've been staring at it for so long and

for whatever reason that you can't seem to put your finger on, it's not good enough to be called "finished" so you keep fucking around with it for the rest of your life. You're searching the depths of the Internet doing "market research" and looking for the "right" way to complete the task, and when you can't find the perfect solution that will solve all your issues, you simply give up and say *never mind.* Or I'd better keep looking.

And the perfectionism wins again. Either way, you're not making any progress, are you?

The next time you notice your mind cycling into that perfectionist wheel spinning, I want you to sink in and assess.

What is your inner critic saying to you right now? What stories are you believing?

Challenge those negative thoughts and the reasons you're telling yourself as to why you're not making progress or why you're not ready/perfect/good enough/smart enough.

It's so easy to get stuck in that all-or-nothing thinking, too. Like, "I'm either a success or a failure," when really there's a shit ton of room in between.

Lemme tell you this right now: *You are worthy because of who you are, not what you've accomplished.*
It's not black or white.
It's not good versus bad.
It's messy and imperfect and beautiful.

*Just like you.*

I don't know who needs to hear this, but there's no ONE right way to do anything. *(What's that saying, there's more than one way to skin a cat? Why is that a thing?)*

*The right way to do something is the way that works for you.* Fuck what everyone else is doing.

It's time to do things YOUR way.

So what do you say?

Fuck perfectionism.

Choose to start now.

Start your business.

Start loving your body.

Start a new habit.

Start setting boundaries.

Start prioritizing your time.

Start crushing your dreams.

Start forgiving yourself.

Start having fun.

*Just start.*

Take the leap, friend.

You've got this.

(And I've got you!)

That clarity and "readiness" you're looking for is built through action, not the other way around. So the next time you're at a crossroads and staring perfectionism in the face, remember this:

*The intersection of SOMEDAY and NEXT TIME is NEVER.*

Perfect doesn't exist.
But you do.

*How magical!*

## Fuck Perfection Affirmation

*I allow myself to make mistakes because I know that they're op-portunities for growth.*

## Fuck Perfection Exercise

1.  How does perfectionism show up for you?
2.  What do you believe you need to work through right now in order to begin to release this?

# GIVE YOURSELF
# PERMISSION TO SUCK

The main character of every movie goes through this glow up where, when they start out, they're so freakin' terrible at what they're doing.

I'm picturing every single cheesy ice-skating or gymnastics movie ever made right now, where the main characters give themselves permission to suck and go after their dreams of winning the championship trophy. And we don't judge them for their initial suckiness, do we?

As a matter of fact, we LIVE for their journey.

It's literally the entire movie.

So, why do we judge ourselves?

Here's the thing. No one is watching you as closely as you are watching you.

People don't care.

They're worried about their own shit; they don't have time to worry about yours.

I started going to CrossFit recently.

(If you would have asked me a year ago if I'd ever be a "CrossFitter," I would have laughed in your face. I mean, for starters, I was pregnant at the time, but I also never pictured myself working out with a bunch of people who were better than me. Sounds fucking horrible; count me out.)

But here we are.
It's been a journey full of "firsts."
You know, my first rope climb.
My first wall walk.
My first double under.
My first toes-to-bar.

I think a lot about my journey to where I am now while I'm working out, and how it relates to coaching and running a business.

I could have waited to join a CrossFit gym until I was "more fit" and knew how to do all the movements.

I could have waited to show the world any of my progress until I was "good at it."

Or I could have quit because it was pretty damn clear that everybody else was better than me and maybe the world doesn't need another wannabe CrossFit athlete.

But that's the thing with life and business.
You gotta start somewhere.

*Before* you're ready.
Because "ready" never comes.
There will always be *one more thing* you feel like you need to do or finish before you can go after whatever it is that truly matters to you.

Basically anything I've ever done, I did before I was ready.

- *Left my corporate 9-5*
- *Built an online lettering course for beginners*
- *Created a printable hand-lettered coloring book full of positive affirmations*
- *Launched a group coaching program*
- *Invested in a coach*
- *Started offering 1:1 coaching*
- *Spoke at a summit about confidence as an entrepreneur*
- *Created an online course about boundaries*
- *Spoke on podcasts as an expert guest*
- *Joined a coaching certification program*
- *Hosted my first stand-up comedy show for charity*
- *Had a baby*
- *Wrote a damn book.*

And you know how I did it? I trusted in myself and my abilities to show up and do the damn thing for the greater good of my dreams for my life and business.

Don't get me wrong; there was plentyyyyy of self-doubt. In the beginning, I cried pretty much every other week about how difficult and overwhelming everything was.

I once cried into a bowl of oatmeal on a Sunday morning watching *Pioneer Woman* because I had big decisions to make before Monday.

Yeah—leaving your comfort zone is tough.
*We know that.*

But so is staying in it.

Here's the truth: You're probably never going to feel completely ready.

To ask for that promotion.

To leave your comfort zone.

To quit your 9–5.

To hire a coach.

There always will be that little voice in the back of your mind that's afraid and trying to "protect" you. *(Thanks for the help, self-doubt, but we've got dreams to chase!)*

I remember the first time I invested in a coach. I nearly shit my pants when they told me the investment: $6000!

I didn't have the money, and fuck, I was SCARED. But I could SEE the next/better/happier version of me, and I knew I needed their help to get there.

So I decided I was going to make it work, no matter what it took, and I signed up.

And you know what happened?

My life changed.

My business grew.

And my confidence skyrocketed.

And everything I learned from that coach helped me pay for the program, like magic.

Looking back, I'm able to laugh at how afraid I was to invest in myself. It was 100% worth it, and I haven't stopped investing since.

So today, my friend, as you're reading this, I want you to ask yourself—what are you not doing because you're afraid to suck?

*And how can you do it anyway?*

How can you become an expert, achieve your goals, or conquer that mountain if you never try? Trust that the universe has your back, give yourself permission to suck for the sake of growth, and take that uncomfortable leap of faith towards your dreams.

I literally fucking sucked at CrossFit when I first started, yet I showed up anyways and *continued* to show up.

And you know what?

I got better at it. *(Should they make a CrossFit movie about me?)*

I'm curious. When was the last time you gave yourself permission to suck at something? For the sake of doing the damn thing.

That's CrossFit for me. My goal when I first started going to the gym was to go two times a week.

Those two times a week turned into three times a week and then five times a week and before I knew it, I felt comfortable in the gym.

Don't get me wrong, I don't look "good" doing any of the movements—you could compare me to that of a wet noodle trying to flip a stick around, more on this later LOL—but it *feels* good, and I'm proud of myself for putting in the work.

I gave myself permission to suck at CrossFit, and through it, I've gained friends, improved my self-confidence, and learned many a lesson that I've been able to apply to my coaching business.

So I want you to ask yourself—what is that thing that you need to give yourself permission to suck at in order to make progress towards your dreams?

Whether it's public speaking, showing up on video, writing a book, or professional ice-skating, ask yourself: What's my first step?

Think about it like this: *Everything you've ever done, was once something you'd never done.*

You weren't automatically good at shaving your legs the first time you did it. In fact, I'd be willing to put a good amount of money down that you cut the shit out of the front and back of your kneecaps the first few times.

And now look at you, all hairless and shit.

It's the same concept with your dreams and goals.

*Practice makes progress.*

Notice I didn't say practice makes perfect.

Perfect is a lie, remember? *(Unless you're Ryan Gosling. Hi, Ryan.)*

**Give yourself permission to fuck around and find out.**

We weren't just innately born with the ability to play the piano, sink free-throws under pressure, or land an Axel jump on the ice. *(I shit you not, I literally just Googled "hard ice skating move.")*

We had to practice.

We had to suck at it.

(We also had to keep sucking at it for a while.)

And that's totally okay.

No one expected you to come out of the womb walking around and playing Mozart, just like no one expects you to be good at something you've never done before.

You are a beautiful work in progress, and you must see yourself as such.

Just like the main character in every story, there will come a time when you decide that the cost of staying where you currently are is greater than the discomfort of starting something new and working towards what truly matters to you.

**"And the day came when the risk to remain tight in a bud was more painful than the risk it took to blossom."**

*~ Anais Nin*

And when that time comes, it might feel scary, but hot damn it's going to feel good to take action, isn't it?

*Maybe that's what this chapter, and what life, is all about.*

The fearless action.
The bold determination.
The unrelenting pursuit of the things that mean the most.

You can sit around and talk about your dreams all day long, but until you make the courageous decision to put pen to paper, say yes to yourself, and start taking those baby steps—regardless of how scary or uncomfortable it all feels—you will remain in the exact same place you are now.

So what's it gonna be, friend?

You gonna talk about it or you gonna be about it?

I don't know about you, but the idea that if I chose to do nothing, I might be in the exact same place a year from now doesn't sit well with me.

That's not Main Character Energy.

That's Bella Swan in the second(?) *Twilight* when Edward leaves her and the movie depressingly goes on without her for months while she sits in her bedroom staring out the window.

You are here because you know you were made for more.

You were meant to do more.

Be more.

And have more.

And that kind of person doesn't play small, do they?

*It's time to go suck.*

## Give Yourself Permission to Suck Affirmation

*I give myself permission to try new things, even if I'm not immediately good at them.*

## Give Yourself Permission to Suck Exercise

1. Brain dump five areas you could give yourself permission to suck for the sake of progress towards your dreams.

2. Choose one.

3. *Fucking do it.*

# KNOW YOUR REASONS WHY

Lemme be real with you.

I've almost given up at least a hundred times.

Running my own business is the second-most magical thing I've ever done. (After having a baby, of course.)

Magical, because:

I've found my calling.

I love helping people.

I'm changing lives.

I control my schedule.

I get (and get paid) to help humans build self-love, create badass boundaries, and get out of their own way so they can boost productivity, let go of limiting beliefs, and be unapologetically themselves. My clients are confidently creating the fulfilling and impactful lives and businesses they've been dreaming of—without second-guessing their abilities.

And I couldn't be more proud and honored.

On the other hand... It's a lot.

People talk about entrepreneurship being tough, but I didn't understand until I was in it. (Literally the same with motherhood. There's nothing anyone could have told me that would have actually prepared me for the next-level shit it is to grow, birth, feed, and raise a new human.)

In my opinion, you're never truly ready for any of it. Because ready is a lie, remember? When business gets tough, you figure it out. When your baby is crying, you figure it out. When something keeps digging up the onions you planted in your garden, you set up cameras and plot the demise of whatever creature is betraying your integrity. One way or a fucking 'nother, you figure. It. Out.

Every problem has a solution, and everything is figure-outable. We dive in and find solutions because the problems matter to us.

I host a virtual stand-up comedy show for charity every year benefiting a mental health nonprofit because mental health awareness, support, and resources are important to me.

I coach because I believe everyone should feel seen and heard for who they truly are—not who they feel like they have to be.

And I'm writing a book because I want you to embrace your Main Character Energy and experience the joy, power, and peace of leading a life with confidence and authenticity.

*What matters to YOU?*

Whatever answer came to your mind, and I want that first impulse answer, not the logical, thought-out one, *that's why you're here.* That's why you get up in the morning. Your purpose. Your calling.

There's an exercise from Dean Graziosi's book, *Millionaire Success Habits,* called the Seven Levels Deep Exercise, and it's a helpful tool to help you uncover your why and the driving force behind every decision you make in life and/or business.

I'm paraphrasing, but it starts with the question:

1. What do you want to do or achieve in life? And then proceeds to dig deeper....
2. Why is that important to you? And you answer that.
3. Why is THAT important to you? And you answer that.

And it goes even deeper for seven levels until you're at the root of all of it.

Which sounds so fucking simple, but honestly, it's truly thought-provoking and potentially difficult to tap into these answers from your heart instead of your head.

Identifying and understanding your Deepest, Biggest Why is like unlocking the secret to peace. You know, deep down, that you'll always have a golden light inside of you, guiding you to make decisions that align with this core desire inside your soul.

Your Why is there to support you along your path to Main Character Energy, and your best life.

When you feel like giving up—when things feel difficult—remember your Why.

Why are you doing this?

My Why is to help people feel seen and heard for who they truly are, to spread light everywhere I go, and to share the magic I see within.

When I take a moment to remember my Why, it allows me to take a pause, recenter, and release what's holding me back from making aligned and empowered decisions.

Because of my Why, I'm learning to let perfection go. Spinning my wheels and hanging on to projects and ideas because they're "not good enough" isn't serving anyone. In fact, some would argue that it's selfish for me to *not* share my message and help the world in my unique way. Imagine if I had never published this book because it wasn't "perfect." What if my message, that I'd deemed not worthy because it's difficult, is exactly what someone needs to hear at this moment in time?

I gave up working on this book many times.

I hit blocks. I got tired of staring at my computer screen. My baby was crying. My lower back fucking hurt. There were so many reasons I didn't want to finish this book, but all it took, when those gremlins took over, was a mental re-set and a reminder of why I was writing it in the first place.

If I had forgotten my Why, this book wouldn't be in your hands right now, would it?

Seriously, thanks for reading this—you're the real MVP. My hopes are that, by now, you're feeling grateful I let go of perfection and hit "publish" even when it was fucking scary. If you find yourself having a good time, catching some powerful gold nuggets, and/or resonating with these lessons, I'd be eternally grateful if you took a quick moment to leave a review on Amazon so we can help more people around the world step into their Main Character Energy. Thanks so much.

I'm here on this planet to help beautiful humans like you level the fuck up and step into your power. No more hiding. No more dimming your light or shrinking to make others more comfortable. No more settling for less. No more what if'ing.

Every time you don't give up, every time you choose to re-member your Why and see the learnings and lessons instead of accepting defeat, YOU ARE SHOWING THE FUCK UP, AND YOU ARE LEVELING THE FUCK UP.

You are embracing your Main Character Energy.

So keep the focus, my friend, and when you feel like giv-ing up, remember your Why.

## Know Your Reasons Why Affirmation

*I am here for a reason, and I am exactly where I'm supposed to be.*

## Know Your Reasons Why Exercise

1.  Let's go seven levels deep. Take your time and answer EACH one of these.
    *a) What do you want to do/achieve in your lifetime?*
    *b) Why is that important to you?*
    *c) Cool, why is that important to you?*
    *d) Awesome. Why is THAT important to you?*
    *e) Oooh, interesting. Why is that important to you?*
    *f) And what's important to you about that?*
    *g) Great. Now even deeper, why is THAT important to you?*

2.  Reflect on how this exercise went for you. *How are you feeling? Did anything surprise you?*

3.  Now, what are you going to do about this?

# WATCH YOUR MOUTH

You know when you wake up in the middle of the night thinking about something?

That was me with this lesson.

*(I also had that one TikTok song in my head about blue cheese having mold in it.)* Obviously, a great night of sleep.

I don't know why I always wake up thinking about shit (and I truly hate it sometimes), but I like to call 'em intuitive downloads, and I make sure to write them down and share them when they're relevant.

Last night's download was perfect for tapping into your Main Character Energy.

It was about the power of the subconscious mind and how the language we use is an incredible driving force and predictor of the outcomes of certain situations.

As a neurolinguistic programming (NLP) practitioner—which basically means I'm certified in the language of the subconscious mind and how our thoughts affect our behavior—I'm always thinking about thinking.

How meta is that? My brain hurts just thinking about thinking about thinking.

Here's the download: *The way you think and the language you use MATTERS.*

Simple, yet so profound. Because whether you know it or not, you are always using affirmations. Sometimes positive, and sometimes negative. So watch yer mouth, ya filthy animal.

Positive affirmations sound something like this:
*I matter.*
*I have all the time and energy I need to do everything I want to.*
*I am continuously empowering myself to live my best life.*

Powerful, right?

Negative affirmations sound something like this:
*I'm never going to find that special someone.*
*I don't have enough time. Or money. Or energy.*
*I'll never lose weight, get that promotion, reach my goals, etc.*

And those make you feel like shit, don't they?

Here's the deal. Your world is a reflection of your thoughts. Whatever you are choosing to think and believe becomes true for you. So tell me, are your affirmations positive or negative? Next time you catch yourself in a negative thought spiral, ask yourself:

1. Are these thoughts true? *Whatever the answer is, whether it's yes or no, (it's usually no), move on to the next question.*

2. How are they not true?

For example, a thought that pops into my head often is that I'm not a very good entrepreneur. (I know, right?) *insert eye roll emoji here*

I'm constantly having to stop and ask myself: Is this true? What cold-hard evidence do I have to support this negative thought?

Having no incriminating evidence, I move on to the next question.

HOW am I a good entrepreneur? Well shit, I'm glad you asked. I'm booking clients and facilitating massive transformations inside my private coaching containers and the Creating Confidence® Society membership *(seriously, check out heymeganreed.com/society)*, while paying the bills and traveling and spending time with my family. I'm literally getting paid to live my best entrepreneur life. To me, that's evidence this belief is absolutely not true.

Your subconscious mind is always looking for evidence of the thoughts going through your head, so if you're constantly thinking negative thoughts and putting yourself down, saying things like: I suck at hanging on to relationships, I could never make a living doing what I love, I hate how fat I look in that photo, or I can't do this, it's too difficult... you will, in fact, begin to notice how true all that bullshit is for you. And those beliefs will continue to manifest and show up over and over again.

What we draw our attention to becomes our reality.

*Isn't your subconscious mind so powerful?*

Whether you know it or not, you are always affirming beliefs about yourself.

If you start a sentence with an "I" and follow it up with a statement or observation, that's an affirmation—be it positive or negative—and while maybe you're making a joke in passing about how bad you are with money or how you'll never be able to lose that extra fluff you've got in your midsection because that's just the nature of getting older and you had three babies, your subconscious mind is always listening.

The key is to bring awareness to the thoughts you're thinking and the things you're saying when you're talking to yourself.

I don't look like a CrossFitter. *Remember?*
I don't look like any kind of elite athlete, really.

Saturdays at KAMO Athletics CrossFit gym are for partner workouts, and most of the time I don't get to go because 10 a.m. happens to fall during Sonora's first nap.

This particular morning, she slept in until 7:45, and since we had a busy afternoon ahead of us, we knew she'd likely only get one nap, so we decided to push her/wear her out by taking her to the gym in hopes that she'd take one really good nap from like 11:30 a.m.–2:30 p.m.

*(She's currently napping, I'll let you know how it goes.)*

Anyways.

First off, I fucking hate partner workout days because you're immediately taken back to elementary school days during P.E. and recess when you're partnering up for things and you get picked last.

I mean, on one hand, I love the accountability and camaraderie and since I'm a competitive person it generally pushes me to work hard as shit.

But on the other hand, every single time they go over the WOD (workout of the day) and start teaming up, I catch myself looking around the room.

*Everyone here is better than me.*

*No one wants to be my partner.*

You see, in my head, for someone to be my partner would mean they'd have to stoop down to my level. They'd have to wait on me. Never mind the fact that I have limbs longer than proportionally appropriate for a standard human body so I've never been able to do a "real" push up and I look like a baby giraffe who can't pick up their legs when they run. *What a visual, amirite?*

I made varsity in high school because of three reasons: I was tall, I was competitive, and I was coachable. Like sure, I had some athletic ability in there, but you would never know it just by looking at me.

Second off, I've got my 14-month-old daughter there running around, so I'm probably going to be a little distracted. Some days she plays with her toys and does great during the workout, and other days she's a loose cannon trying to drink from everyone's water cups—if it has a straw, it's fair game—climb the wooden staircase to the loft, or run around the parking lot because the giant garage doors are open. And this close to nap time, you never know what you're gonna get.

Either way, I almost always have to pause my workout and feed/redirect/hang out with her for a bit.

After a quick sweep of the people in the room ready to workout, I begged Brandon to be my partner. It was a leap-frog style workout where we'd take turns doing five different sets of exercises, like when I was out running 400 meters around the building, he'd watch Sonora, and then he'd do the next programmed piece while I watched her—for ten rounds.

"Fine," he says.

We finished the warm up, and I'm already tired and thinking about leaving.

For some reason though, I stayed, and the workout started.

I took off on my 400-meter portion of the run around the cluster of buildings, and as I was running I caught a glimpse of my reflection in a big window and thought, "Wow, you really look stupid."

I had been watching all the other people run past me and in front of me and the power and grace with which they moved. I could feel my inner critic saying: *Bitch, you don't belong here, you don't even look like a CrossFitter, and you're never gonna be one.* And it hurt.

I didn't want to be there anymore.

Literally how embarrassing that I was even there.

I work out for both my mental and physical health, and I'm still trying to figure out my postpartum body (*not to* mention I had a third-degree pelvic prolapse before and after birth so there's a relatively valid underlying fear that my uterus is just going to fall out of my vagina when I'm working out again), so the fact that I was there at all was a win, but fuck, it didn't feel like it as I rounded the corner of the building, watching myself fall farther and farther behind everyone else.

I am so fucking behind.

I should be stronger by now.

I should be able to keep up.

I should work out more often.

I should find a different form of exercise.

Hmm... yoga sounds nice, although there's mirrors in there too and I know for a fact I look awkward as fuck doing yoga, too. Where can I get some of that grace and poise everyone else has?

I should quit.

And the whole time these thoughts are going through my head, I'm noticing them.

In real time, I'm recognizing the fucked-up things my inner critic is saying to me. Cool, Marlene. Welcome to the party. And I'm wondering to myself: What if the things my inner critic says are true?

Nope.

No way.

Stop that shit right now.

Cancel/clear/delete that thought.

And I found myself wishing I had my phone on me so I could make a voice memo and document this whole journey for you. The roller-coaster clusterfuck of me and my ego arguing inside my head during a Saturday CrossFit workout.

I'm always looking inward for inspiration, takeaways, and learnings and how I can make them relatable, shareable, and applicable to you and my clients, and I remember thinking to myself, *"I should put this in my book somewhere, but what chapter would I put it in, and what's the lesson here?"*

It's in this chapter, and here are the lessons:
*Don't give up.*
*Give yourself grace.*
*Quit comparing yourself to others.*
*You do you.*
*Move your body, even if you look stupid.*
*Keep going.*
*Fuck what other people say.*
*Quit projecting your insecurities.*
*Focus on you.*
*No one is watching you as closely as you are watching you.*
*Not everything you think is true.*
*No one cares.*
*Watch your mouth.*

I finished the workout dead last, sweaty and out of breath, and scanned the room. Not a single person was looking at me. No one cared. They were all focused on themselves, and I wondered to myself whether they, too, were also comparing themselves to others and dealing with their inner critic. Or maybe they used to.

And I realized it didn't matter.

What mattered most was how I felt about myself, and the recognition of the negative thoughts and stories I was telling myself. When you're able to recognize—especially in the moment—negative self-talk, that story begins to lose its power.

I'm not saying it doesn't still hurt, because it sure fucking does, but the self-awareness piece is crucial for overcoming and rewriting it. Because in that moment, when you can zoom out and notice yourself having that conversation, you can identify what you're truly needing in that moment.

For me, I needed to quit comparing myself to others, I needed to give myself grace, and I needed to keep going, no matter what the voice in my head was saying.

*P.S. It's 12:55 p.m., and I can hear that Sonora's awake in her crib. So much for a three-hour nap LOL.*

So let's bring awareness to the thoughts we're thinking. Where do you need to watch your language?

For me, six phrases that immediately send up a red flag and alert my logical mind that I might be telling my subconscious mind a limiting story are:

1) *I can't...*
2) *I have to...*
3) *I'm never...*
4) *I'm not...*
5) *I don't...*
6) *I should...*

When you speak to yourself in negatives and limiting beliefs, there's a possibility you're leaving important and necessary personal growth on the table. Don't get me wrong—there's totally a time and place to say you can't do something, but in my experience, we're quick to say it without truly assessing the situation.

Let's take a look at a few things you could say instead to help shift your mindset. These reframes are helpful prompts to challenge your mind to think positively and look for solutions outside the box *(and outside your comfort zone)*.

## Subconscious Language Reframes

*1) How can I _____?*

Don't declare defeat that easily by saying you can't do something. Turn it around and make it actionable. How can you make it work? How can you do that thing? What is one small step you can take action on towards this thing you "can't" do?

This phrase, "How can I _____," lets your subconscious mind know that you believe there are solutions to the problem at hand, and in my experience, simply acknowledging there's a solution brings you one step closer to finding it. What floats to your awareness may surprise you.

*2) I won't _____.*

Be honest. Is it something you really can't do, or is it something you just *won't* do? It's totally fine if you won't do it, but that's a decision you're making. You are choosing to not do that thing. For example: I say I can't have gluten at restaurants because the waiters are more likely to take me seriously, but technically, I could have it. Terrible, painful things will happen (thanks, Crohn's), but my decision to give up gluten in 2017 was an empowered choice, and because I care about my health, I won't have it.

This phrase, "I won't _____," gives you your power back.

*3) I get to _____.*

We say it all the time... "I have to." What if instead of HAVING to do something, we GET to do something? And let's be real here, I know there are certain things you simply *have* to do, but what if there was actually something positive to be found in the mix? Let's rewrite a few that I see often:

You have to go to work.
*You GET to go to work. You are grateful for the income that supports you and your family.*

You have to go to the gym.
*You GET to go to the gym and move your body. How amazing to commit to your physical and mental health!*

You have to go grocery shopping.
*You GET to provide your body with sustenance and energy. You are so grateful for the money to purchase what you need.*

You have to take care of your sick family member.
*You GET to spend time with your loved one, even if it's difficult.*

Imagine choosing the latter statements. Holy shift, right? I help my clients recognize and rewrite thought patterns—just like these—that are keeping them from living their dream life and finding their joy.

### 4) *I'm still learning _____.*

This one's a big one for me with food. I was raised in a good old-fashioned, meat-and-potatoes farm family, so naturally, I grew up a relatively picky eater. I've expanded my palette a shit ton since graduating college, but there are still a few foods I can't seem to get on board with. Because I want to like all* foods, I'm careful not to say "I hate cucumbers," and instead say, "I'm still learning to like cucumbers." *I do not care to ever like celery. It's truly the fucking worst.*

I'm hoping, as I model this language in front of our daughter, she'll be more open and willing to try foods in the future she maybe didn't love the first time she was exposed to them.

The phrase "I'm still learning _____" is an incredibly powerful rewrite because it's telling your subconscious mind that you will, in fact, learn how to do that thing that you previously told yourself you couldn't do.
*I'm still learning how to love and accept myself.*
*I'm still learning the ins and outs of technology.*
*I'm still learning how to write a fucking book.*

Your belief in yourself and your ability to succeed is, in my opinion, one of the biggest predictors of said success.

*If you believe you can, you bet your sweet ass you can.*

If you believe you can't, you won't.

You can do anything you set your mind to, my friend.

*You can lead a life with confidence and authenticity, as easily and effortlessly as you decide to.*

## Watch Your Mouth Affirmation

*Whatever I choose to think and believe becomes true for me.*

## Watch Your Mouth Exercise

1.  Brain dump ten (or more) limiting/negative thoughts, beliefs, or stories you've been telling yourself.

2.  Cross them out and rewrite them into more positive statements using the subconscious language reframes.

3.  Next time you catch yourself in a negative thought spiral, ask yourself:
    *a) Are these thoughts true?*
    *b) How are they not true?*
    *c) What small shift can I take in a positive direction?*

# SEEK INTERNAL VALIDATION

There was a time in my life when I didn't know who I was.

I mean, I had no idea at the time that I didn't know who I was—that level of meta self-awareness had not yet been unlocked—but what I did know was that I was living every single day in a general state of unhappiness.

I didn't know what alignment or values were, but I knew something was off.

My parents were the best parents they knew how to be, our relationship was and is great, and I love them dearly, but objectively looking back on my childhood knowing what I know now, I had a lot of emotional needs that went unmet.

Imagine it in a big headline on the cover of a satire *Onion* article:

### "RURAL FARM FAMILY AVOIDS FEELINGS"
*With a conservative picture of a mom, dad, and three kids smiling while standing in a field of crops or posing in front of a tractor, barn, or other farm equipment/animals.*

If you grew up in the Midwestern United States, this headline and photo just made you laugh. Relatable, right?

You know exactly what I'm talking about. If you didn't, let me fill you in on the cultural norms in the middle of no-where, U-S-of-A.

Good grades = expected.

Rest = lazy.

Church = go.

People pleasing = standard practice.

Boundaries = never heard of them.

Hard work = good.

Emotions = bad.

Other than the idea that you should "work hard and help others and make an honest living," nothing in my child-hood was normalized. I didn't see my parents express emotions or argue or love on each other. I still remember when my maternal grandfather died when I was in the fifth grade, I never even saw my mom cry about it. I saw her "have a headache" and escape to her room.

I grew up in an environment where it felt unsafe to express emotions because I believed it was wrong to have them in the first place.

I'm finding this come up for me now too, as a mom, an old trigger from my past. I don't want my daughter to feel pain or experience anger or sadness, and it's taking every-thing in me to recognize that my first instinct is to distract her from the pain rather than allow her to feel what she's feeling and help her know that she is safe, supported, and her feelings are valid.

So it makes total sense why I would have struggled with depression growing up. Rather than allowing myself to feel my feelings, I shoved them down.

And each time I shoved something down, I would feel a sense of shame, and I'd hear my inner critic tell me I was inherently a worthless embarrassment of a human because I had all these feelings that no one else did.

In an effort to connect to myself, I craved validation from others. Which sounds like it should make absolutely zero sense, but in hindsight it actually totally tracks. With the voices in my head telling me I wasn't good enough, I wasn't beautiful, I wasn't smart enough, I didn't matter, and that people didn't love me, I needed someone *else* to make me feel worthy.

My soul was begging for deep connection.

I sought external validation and approval in an effort to receive the love and emotions I so desperately craved to feel within myself. *I didn't know how to feel them, remember?*

I needed people to tell me they liked me. That I was funny, smart, or beautiful.

I always had a boyfriend. I always got good grades. I participated in everything. I won awards. Teachers liked me. I fit in everywhere.

But it was never enough.
*I* *was never enough.*

Because validation, when from an external source, only lasts as long as your favorite perfume. It's strong at first, and smells so fucking good, but by the end of the day it's faint—if it's even there at all—because it's faded and you've gone nose blind to it so you find yourself needing to apply it again and again to be able to notice that same delicious smell from when you first put it on.

Internal validation is the concept that YOU are the only one who gets to recognize, decide, and affirm the way you feel about yourself, independent of external factors such as other people's dumb-ass opinions or stupid societal expectations.

*The perfume analogy doesn't work for this one LOL.*
Or maybe it does. Let's try it.

With internal validation, we don't feel the need or desire to even wear perfume because the natural scent of our body is perfectly acceptable to us.
Oh, that totally works.

External validation: "You smell good."
You blush, smile, say thanks, and get a quick release of dopamine and oxytocin (two feel-good hormones) that fade over time.

Internal validation: "I smell good."
This inner knowing, that you are worthy whether or not someone compliments you for the cloud of fragrance you bathed in this morning, is a lasting feeling of peace and

self-acceptance that goes much deeper than a positive comment from a stranger at the airport.

Which makes sense, why I never felt good for very long. I was thrill-seeking affection and approval from others through flirty texts and casual hookups which, in the end, left me feeling disappointed and lonely because what I was really looking for was love and validation from myself.

The story that I was telling myself was that I didn't belong anywhere.

*There's a difference between fitting in and belonging.*

Brené Brown, an American professor and best-selling author known for her work on shame and vulnerability, perfectly describes the difference between the two in her book *Gifts of Imperfection.* She says,

"Fitting in is about assessing a situation and becoming who you need to be to be accepted. Belonging, on the other hand, doesn't require us to change who we are; it requires us to be who we are."

I "fit in" because I could blend and morph myself into whoever I needed to be. Real chameleon-type shit where I was physically there, but felt like no one ever saw the real me.

I never felt like I "belonged" because I wasn't showing up as my true self.

It's taken a lot of grace and forgiveness as an adult to let go of my past and embrace who I was when I didn't know who that person was. To be fair, I was young, and my prefrontal cortex wasn't fully formed yet.

I didn't believe I was worthy of self-love.
*Shit, I didn't even know what self-love was.*

I wasted a lot of time in my past disliking who I was and what I looked like and I've watched my clients spend a lot of time disliking pieces of themselves, too.

I was lost.

And the key to finding myself was awareness.

Awareness really is the key to all of it, isn't it?

When you become aware of the underlying needs behind your desire for external validation, it gives you your power back. Because had I known, when I was younger, that I was craving a deeper love and acceptance for who I truly was, I could have saved myself so many years of approval-seeking, embarrassment, and heartache.

*No regrets, though. I learned some important-ass lessons, and everything that's ever happened is part of my personal journey and life story.*

While I don't wish to go back and change any of my experiences, there are some learnings that I've taken away since then that I want to share with you, in case you need to hear them:

*Some people will like you, some people won't, and that's okay.*
*You are not for everyone, and not everyone is for you.*
*It's safe to have feelings and express your emotions.*

*And it's okay to be yourself, even if you're different from everyone else.*

This seems so stupidly simple, but no one ever told me this. Like, really told me—to the point where I heard it, believed it, and embodied it. I literally had no idea I could just \*bE mYseLf\* even though there were posters hanging all over my high school about it.

The world needs variety. That's what makes you exciting and fun and unique and lovable.

*That's what makes you the main character.*

The ice-cream shop has thirty different flavors, and some people like the peanut butter chocolate chip, and some like the vegan vanilla, and both flavors are worthy of love and they don't try to be like the other flavor because they know and accept who they are.

You are someone's favorite flavor of ice cream.

*\*Blatantly ignores the fact that you are also someone's least favorite flavor of ice cream because their opinion of ice-cream flavors is none of your business. As long as you like your flavor, that's all that fucking matters.\**

Showing up with authenticity and loving who you truly are—whether you're butterscotch or strawberry or mint chocolate chip or you've got nuts—LOL—is a crucial key for showing up with confidence.

*Because here's the thing:*

**You cannot hate yourself into a version of you that you love.**

117

It just doesn't work that way. If you want to love yourself, you must first allow yourself to feel worthy of being loved.

You are so worthy, damnit. And deep down, you know it, don't you?

You're the fucking main character.

Everyone loves the main character, quirks and all. Even the main characters that you're not sure about in the beginning of the show, but when you start getting to know them it turns out they're an incredible person with a unique story.

*This is you.*

An incredible human with a unique story who gets to decide that you are worthy, just as you are. No one else can decide this for you.

Remember when I said your subconscious mind is always listening? When you release the need to fit in and be liked and validated by others, you're allowing your brain to be cool with YOU, just the way you are. Validating and accepting our own being allows us to be true to our authentic selves, feel like we belong, and live according to our own core values and beliefs.

That's the dream, isn't it?
Main Character Energy AF.

The pressure to fit in is off, friend.
*You already belong.*

## Seek Internal Validation Affirmation

*I am worthy, valuable, and confident in who I am and my place in this world.*

## Seek Internal Validation Exercises

1.  Where in your life (or business) do you seek external validation?

2.  What is your soul asking for? *What do you truly need?*

# YOU CAN'T POUR
# FROM AN EMPTY CUP

You've heard this saying before, haven't you?
You can't pour from an empty cup.

I mean, you can totally try to pour from an empty cup—
*and we do this all the time, don't we?*—but what value are you
adding to anyone's lives if you're pouring and pouring and
trying to pour some more but nothing's coming out?

Then all of a sudden you're resentful and depleted and IF
on the off chance you were able to pour from some secret
and magical reserve, now you're burnt out, and your battery
is drained as fuck.

You're literally so exhausted that instead of taking a regular ol' eight hours of sleep to recharge your battery, you
can't even get out of bed for two weeks.

It's a classic story line in the movie industry. You could
describe hundreds of movies these days with this *New York
Times* headline: **"MAIN CHARACTER OVERWHELMED,
LOSES THEIR SHIT."**

Let's take a look at the main character in the Disney classic, *Frozen.*

In case you've never seen it—*seriously where the fuck have you been?*—the movie tells the story of two sisters, Elsa and Anna, and their struggles to navigate their relationship amid Elsa's growing magical powers.

Elsa has the power to create cold shit like snow and ice, but because she struggles to control it, she isolates herself from her sister and the rest of society. She pours all of her energy into keeping her powers and true self hidden so she can protect herself from the judgment of others.

However, as the movie progresses, Elsa cracks. She hits such a breaking point that she runs away so she can be herself and wear sexy dresses and sing and recharge her batteries alone in a castle she built out of ice.

She realizes that she can't keep pouring from an empty cup, and that in order to overcome her fears of judgment and control her powers, she needs to embrace her true self, take a damn break, and seriously prioritize some self-care.

In the scene where Elsa sings the hit song, "Let It Go," as she builds her ice castle, she finally releases her fears and embraces her true self. She sheds her old persona of the perfect princess and steps into her power—choosing to live her life on her own terms.

Throughout the rest of the movie, Elsa learns to control her powers and uses them to help her sister and save her kingdom. And in doing so, she discovers a sense of inner strength and peace that she had been missing.

The lessons and reminders that you can't pour from an empty cup are powerful themes in movies like *Frozen*, because they serve as helpful lil' reminders that in order to overcome our fears and embrace our true selves, we must prioritize self-care and take care of our own needs.

*(Another great example of this story in a movie is* The Pursuit of Happyness, *which I only recommend if you're looking for a good ugly cry.)*

You must prioritize self-care.

When your phone goes into low-power mode, you plug it in, right?.

When YOU go into low-power mode, you have a choice. You can either buckle down and push through and squeeze out every last bit of energy you have in you, or you can take a moment, step away from the shit show, and recharge your battery.

Charged batteries perform better.

It's science.

You want to help people.

I know. I get it. I want to do the same thing.

But tell me—who are you going to be able to help if you're drained and overwhelmed?

Imagine with me, that you have a beautiful red plastic cup.

When you're rested and recharged, your cup is full of liquid. *(What's your liquid? My first instinct was to say champagne but honestly, just gimme a Starbucks Pink Drink and I'm all set.*

*Ain't nobody want a cup full of champagne every day, and if you do, you might want to talk to somebody about it.)*

Back to the cup of liquid.

This liquid is your energy, your life force, your time.

When it's full, you have so much to give to others. You can literally be like Oprah with it if you want. "You get some liquid, YOU get some liquid!"

But you find, as the day goes on and you're pouring into other people's cups, that you're getting kind of thirsty. So you go to take a drink, only your cup is empty. *Have you ever woken up after a night with a stuffy nose and your mouth is so dry but when you grab your water bottle and tip it back, it's empty except for one little drop that barely does anything? That's what I'm imagining here.*

Your cup is empty, because you've been pouring into everyone else's all day long without stopping to refill yours.

You must make time for things that charge your battery.
That fill your cup up.
Okay, so I'm mixing my metaphors. You get it.

You MUST rest, and you must make time for play and for creative, life-giving activities. Rest is one of the most productive things you can do for your cup.

And I'm not talking about the kind of rest where you lie on the couch and scroll social media for three hours. That's not rest, that's numbing.

What *is* rest, then?

I'm not sure I knew what rest was growing up.

I went to a relatively small rural school with about seventy kids in my graduating class, so it was totally normal to do *literally every activity.*

Not a single person questioned the fact that I was the yearbook co-editor, journalism photographer, played varsity volleyball, basketball, and softball, had leading roles in the school's theater productions, sang in the choir, participated in Forensics and Scholar's Bowls, was the secretary of Students Against Drunk Driving (SADD), president of the girl's club, spent evenings at rehearsal for a musical a town over, had show pigs in the county fair, took college credit classes early, had a 4.0 GPA, or was a teacher's aide. Not to mention I had time for a boyfriend who lived an hour away.

No one questioned that?

It's no wonder it took me so long to release the incessant need to be working all the time and doing all the things.

To rest was to be lazy.

Sometimes I wonder who I'd be today if I had gone to a bigger school where you had to choose one activity and run with it, or actually set boundaries around your time and energy.

We're raised in a hustle culture—because to be busy means you're "a really good person contributing to society" and to say no would mean you're a heartless brat.

You ever been in a conversation with someone who asked you to do something and you said yes instinctively before even giving yourself a chance to think about it? (Your boss, your colleague, your neighbor, your client, your family, your partner...?)

The *"sure, no problem"* just word-vomited outta you.

And immediately you were filled with annoyance/dread/guilt/regret/shame, wishing you could go back and change your answer.

Why do we do that? Why do we say yes when we want to say no?

I'll tell you.

It's because we've been programmed to "put others first," and damn it, we're fucking professionals at it, aren't we?

I'm taking a real shot in the dark here, but I'm guessing that—out of obligation—you said yes because you've got a habit of people pleasing and overcommitting due to a lack of solid boundaries. *Because if you say no, that little voice inside your head would call you selfish, right?*

If you're finding yourself in scenarios where you're feeling *some type of way*—you know, like there's a pit in your stomach, a burning in your chest, a lump in your throat, or your cup has 8,000 little holes in it and you can't seem to keep going at this rate—it's time to evaluate your boundaries.

*Because busyness is not a flex, burnout isn't a badge of honor, and you simply cannot pour from an empty cup.*

If you're overwhelmed and constantly stressed when it comes to your life, business, and career, you don't have *pAsSiOn* for helping others, you have a lack of boundaries.

There's a difference between a season of hard work to accomplish something on a deadline vs. a pattern of working late nights and weekends, taking on more than you can handle, and missing out on life events and holidays because you're "too busy" working.

I don't know about you, but I'm curating my life to SUPPORT my dreams and goals, not hinder them.

*Imagine what better boundaries could do for the quality of your life (and business).*
*Imagine getting to hang more with friends and family.*
*Imagine relaxing in the evenings instead of hustling.*
*Imagine having time for the things that truly matter to you.*
*Imagine creating a deeper impact in the lives of those around you.*

It's 100% possible for you.

And I know what you're thinking.

One, you're not even sure where to start, and two, you're worried what people will say. And maybe you're even getting a little sweaty about the idea of a confrontational conversation where you might have to say no to someone or something.

I get it, I totally do.

127

You want to make others happy—it's in your nature, isn't it?—so you say yes to everything out of fear/guilt/shame.

Fear you'll hurt the relationship.

Guilt that they're "family," so you're obligated to be at every event.

Shame around putting yourself first.

Lemme be real clear with you here:

*The only people who think setting boundaries is selfish are the ones who were benefiting from you having none.*

Read that again.

There are people out there, whether intentionally or un-intentionally—it doesn't really matter—that will poke holes in your cup. They'll take energy from you, and they'll drain you of all your liquid to keep their cups full. Energy vampires.

Whether it's a client that's requesting "one more little thing" before the weekend, a family member that makes passive-aggressive comments about your parenting choic-es, or a colleague that you're always picking up the slack for, you can expect that there will be people in your life that you'll need to regulate and restrict their access to your liquid.

Boundaries, baby.

Because sure, you've got your cup, and they can totally see that, but what's inside it is none of their business.

And because your time is your LIFE.

Just because you have the cup, doesn't mean you have the liquid.

*Just because you have the time, doesn't mean you have the capacity.*

You may not have anything on the calendar for Sunday night, but you know that when you pour liquid and give energy instead of focusing on recharging and planning and preparing for your upcoming week, you start your Monday off frazzled, because your cup's already got a slow leak in it.

*Just because you can, doesn't mean you have to. Or should.*

Just because you can attend all four of your family Thanksgivings in three days doesn't mean you have to. Just because you can take on another little client project real quick doesn't mean you have to. Just because you can run the local holiday fundraiser doesn't mean you have to. Just because you can bake twelve pies for a bake sale—and you're really good at it and everybody loves your damn pies—doesn't mean you have to.

Right here and right now, I want to invite you to take a step back and evaluate the things you're doing because you feel like you have to.

Do you *really* have to?

Sometimes, the answer is yes.

But oftentimes it's just unnecessary pressure you're putting on yourself to pour into everyone else's cups instead of your own.

I want you to ask yourself: Where's that pressure coming from? And how can I release that feeling of obligation and give myself a break?

You don't owe anyone any of your liquid.

You don't owe anyone anything.

Your time, your energy, your resources.

Nothing.

Not a damn thing.

This is going to get spicy, but here's a casual list of people you don't owe your liquid to:

*Your partner.*

*Your boss.*

*Your colleagues.*

*Your clients.*

*Your neighbors.*

*Your siblings.*

*Your small group.*

*Your church/temple/mosque.*

*Your friends.*

*Your family.*

*Your parents.*

Shall I go on, or you get where I'm going, don't you?

Your time and energy is a precious gift.

Give it away—selectively—because you want to.

Not because you have to.

It's YOUR time, get it?

Boss asking you to work late?

Family expecting you to make last-minute plans work?

Clients emailing you with fires to put out over the weekend?

If someone's asking for your liquid, it's either a hell yes or a hell no.

*Or maybe a not right now.*

But hard pass on the obligations and expectations to give them your liquid, my friend.

You see, this is YOUR life, and YOUR story, and YOU get to determine how you spend your time and energy.

Who and what you give your liquid to is your choice.

I can see the triggered mass of old people, with their sharpened pitchforks and fiery torches, coming for me now.

Shouting some kind of bullshit like, "You should give your family your time—ESPECIALLY your parents—because they raised you, and they love you, so you'd damn well better drop everything whenever they need you regardless of what you have going on and how much liquid is in your cup."

*I'm not afraid of you, angry mob. I was burned at the stake in a past life. And I'm baaaack.*

Sure, you absolutely CAN.

But you don't HAVE TO. You are not required to set yourself on fire to keep others warm.

You are 100% worthy of self-love, and boundaries are a huge form of that.

Once I started setting boundaries, I got my time and energy back, gained more confidence, and was able to love myself for who I really was without all the second guessing. *You can 100% have this, too.*

Because here's the thing, you are not a selfish bitch for saying no.

Let's release that story. If someone's saying that about you, you don't have to identify with that. You're an empowered human saying YES to what matters most to you, and you are not responsible for other people's happiness.

You're responsible for your own.

Your boundaries are there to protect you from feeling overwhelmed, stressed, anxious, drained, and resentful.

*I'm making an intentional effort to stay as high-level as possible about boundaries, knowing some day in the near future I'll be writing an entire book about boundary setting and the energetics behind them. If you want more now because you're impatient and love immediate gratification—we are the same—check out my signature boundaries course, "The Badass Boundaries Blueprint" at heymeganreed.com/BBB.*

If you've got the capacity, cool. Share your liquid with those around you.

If you don't, you don't.

Repeat after me: Just because I have the TIME, does not mean I have the CAPACITY.

Your energy is sacred.

*Protect your liquid — it's your most valuable resource.*

## You Can't Pour from an Empty Cup Affirmation

*I am worthy of rest, self-love, and boundaries.*

## You Can't Pour From An Empty Cup Exercises

1. How's your battery level these days? Where's the liquid in your cup? How can you prioritize rest and self-care? *Schedule an activity that's fun, fulfilling, and recharging into your calendar right now.*

2. Who or what is poking holes in your red plastic cup?
   a) *What can you do to protect your energy?*
   b) *Where can you set better boundaries?*

# SLOW PROGRESS
# IS STILL PROGRESS

Slow progress is still progress.
Slow progress is still progress.
*Slow progress is still fucking progress.*

When we have big dreams, we want to achieve them ASAP, don't we? I'm a results-driven kinda gal, so I get a real lady boner for anything instant gratification.

Amazon Prime same-day shipping? Sign me up.

Instacart groceries? Doordash? Deliver that shit.

So when I have to take things slow or learn something new, I hate it. I want what I want, when I want it. Are ya with me?

Maybe that's why this book has taken me so long to write.

"So long..." It's been less than a year since I decided I even wanted to write a book. *insert eye roll emoji here*

It's just taken me longer than I would like.

I want it to be finished already.

I want you to be reading it.

I want to reach more people and change more lives.

I wanna see how cool the cover art looks and whether or not I ended up putting my picture on it. *(Did I?)*

How meta is it that right now I'm writing about finishing my book, and you're reading it, so... I did, in fact, finish the damn thing?

I see this with my clients a lot. And I'm guessing you can relate, too. You're so hard on yourself for not being exactly where you think you're supposed to be right now.
*I should be farther along.*
*I should be making more money by now.*
*I should own a house / be married / have X number of children, cars, podcasts, followers, and swimming pools / *insert your own shoulds here.**

Shoulds are shit.
Any time you're putting pressure on yourself to be someone, somewhere, or something you're not, you're acting out of shoulds and obligations.
You're shoulding all over yourself.
*How weird does the word should look to you right now?*

Slow progress is still progress.

We're so quick to judge ourselves and our shortcomings that we forget to celebrate the journey and each milestone we've achieved along the route.
It may not feel like much at the moment, but every little step forward you take is helping you build momentum on the path towards your goals.

Think of it like a marathon. Every stride you take, no matter how small, brings you closer to the finish line, and you wouldn't expect even the most seasoned runner to sprint twenty-six fucking miles. *Googles how many miles in a marathon to double-check.*

Read that again. Just kidding, don't, because I'm gonna repeat it: *You wouldn't expect even the most seasoned runner to sprint twenty-six miles.*

So how can you expect yourself to cross the finish line of whatever you're working on at a rate quicker than the rate that it takes?

Sure, there are strategies for productivity and time management, but sometimes things just take fucking time, energy, and effort.

And these resources are finite. And life happens, right?

I want my own Netflix comedy special.

And while I understand the principles of manifestation, and I know what's meant for me will not pass me by and it's all happening exactly as it should, I've got a pretty realistic grasp on the idea that I'm probably not going to just wake up tomorrow with an email from Netflix pitching me the deal of a lifetime.

What I do know is that I'm going to continue to take steps towards that dream, no matter how small they feel in the grand scheme of things.

The first step I took towards this goal was to enroll in a six-week stand-up comedy class at the local theater in town. It was terrifying. I straight up ghosted my comfort zone when I attended the first day. We literally dove into the principles of comedy, set a timer and wrote from a prompt the instructor gave us—and performed live in front of the class that day. *My armpits are still sweaty from it.*

At the end of our six weeks, we were supposed to have a live comedy showcase for people to attend—but with the state of the world in 2020, it was canceled.

Not willing to give up on my Netflix dreams, I decided to take matters into my own hands. I was going to have a fucking comedy showcase. I didn't go through six weeks of learning and kissing my comfort zone goodbye just to do nothing with all this kick-assery, so I decided to host a virtual stand-up comedy show for charity.

I set up a fundraiser page, emailed my list of 250 people, marketed it on Facebook, and after thirty minutes of laughs on Zoom, raised over $1200 for To Write Love On Her Arms (TWLOHA), a non-profit organization dedicated to providing mental health resources to those struggling with depression and addiction.

I even tagged Netflix in some of my posts. *(They did not contact me. Rude, but okay.)*

A year later, I hosted another virtual stand-up comedy show for charity. Fresh material, even more laughs, and even more confidence in myself. I've decided to make it a yearly thing because I love it so much.

The next step towards my Netflix comedy special? An IRL open mic night.

The next time we interact after you read this part, will you ask me how this is going? *Thanks.*

You see, slow progress is the foundation of nearly all great achievements. If you're not where you'd like to be right now, I want you to take a step back and examine your journey.

Are you making small steps towards your dreams?

Or are you sitting around and waiting for the dream to happen to you?

Because those are different.

And I think you know that.

*Patience and persistence are two crucial keys to the formula of success in almost every movie—and life—ever created.*

You know the main character in *The Blindside* movie? He sucked at football when he started. He could have just said F this.

How about Amanda Bynes's character in *She's the Man*? She fought to play soccer and get a scholarship, even when things weren't going her way, and she could have just given up after the school cut her team. *(Seriously, though, how were they supposed to be in high school in this movie?)*

And we can't forget Tiana in *The Princess and the Frog.* She could have just thrown in the towel when she faced obstacle after obstacle, but she had her heart set on a goal to open her own restaurant and knew how valuable her incremental progress truly was. She believed in herself and her abilities, and she trusted that the journey was going to be worth it in the end.

Every step, no matter how small, was taking them all one step closer to their destinations.

So release the expectations that it all has to happen right now, and embrace the slow progress and celebrate each and every small victory along the way.

Life's too short to wait for your dreams to just HAPPEN. That's why, around here, we're making moves.

We're taking messy, imperfect action.

We're taking baby steps.

Because we know that slow progress is still progress, and we're willing to do whatever it takes to achieve our goals.

So give yourself grace.

Give others grace, too.

Give yourself grace for not being where you thought you'd be by now. For not getting started sooner. For letting your inner critic hold you back. For spinning your wheels.

Give yourself grace for whatever it is that you've been beating yourself up about.

I'd like to pretend I wrote this book in one sitting. I've been beating myself up about how long it's taking me to write it, when I know how impactful these lessons could be in the right hands.

I'm giving myself grace that after my weekend writing retreat in Holton, I didn't touch this book again for weeks.

It's not that I didn't want to work on it.

I thought about it all the fucking time, actually.

But I have a baby. And a husband. And a dog. And clients. And dishes. And a community to run. And a million and one other excuses why I could have given up on my book... but instead, I'm giving myself grace.

Because there's a big-ass difference between making slow progress and being stuck.

I wasn't stuck while writing my book—although sometimes it felt like it—I was moving at the exact pace I needed in order to make sustainable progress.

I know this book will come out exactly when it's supposed to. And in retrospect, less than a year from the moment I decided to write a book to it being published and out into the world is pretty damn amazing.

So tell me, dear reader. Where do you need to give yourself grace, and what do you need to make that happen?

## Slow Progress Is Still Progress Affirmation

*Slow progress is still progress. I'm exactly where I'm supposed to be.*

## Slow Progress Is Still Progress Exercises

1. Where have you been pressuring yourself to be faster/better/farther along? *List 'em out.*

2. Reflect: Where can you give yourself grace, and what do you need to make that happen?

# FEEL IT TO HEAL IT

You ever try to keep something bottled inside and shoved down in the hopes that it will just go away? Yeah, same.

Unfortunately, it doesn't work like that.

You've got to feel it to heal it.

When we ignore our emotions, they not only sit there and fester inside of us, they're literally inside of you plotting a way to get out. Keep an emotion trapped inside for long enough, and it's going to manifest into something physical.

Does your stomach or throat hurt when you don't speak up about something?

Did your mom get a headache when her dad died instead of crying in front of you when you were in the fifth grade?

Energy in motion stays in motion.

*(What is this, physics class?)*

Emotions are the same way.

*A recognized emotion becomes a released emotion.*

I spent nearly the entirety of my pregnancy with our daughter feeling all the feels. We're talking hormonal nightmares, over here.

Not only was I never the type of person who saw herself as a mother, I wasn't quite sure that I wanted kids at all.

145

So when a three-bottles-of-wine night with Brandon led to the exact thing that makes a baby, you can imagine the fear and anxiety I felt until it was actually time to take a pregnancy test. *(I took many, many tests that month. I was freaking out.)*

I spent the entire month mentally preparing myself for what could be a giant identity shift. Who was I to be a mom? How was I going to raise a child? What would this mean for my business? In retrospect, I realize how naive it was of me to panic and assume that I'd get pregnant on the first fuck-up of our twelve years of having sex, but it does happen to people, and I'm like, really lucky.

But when the results kept coming back negative and my period came, I remember being disappointed.

*Maybe I really do want to be a mom.*

This was a big self-awareness moment for me. For my entire life, I'd never pictured myself as a mom because I'd never pictured myself living this long. Thirty years old? Nah. I was *sure* depression would have taken me by then.

And on top of that, my inner critic was so certain that I wouldn't be good at motherhood—that I didn't have a motherly bone in my body—that I'd dismissed the idea of having a family because I wasn't interested in pursuing something I knew I would suck at. *Talk about a fucking limiting belief, am I right?*

So we started pulling the goalie and letting the Universe take the lead. We were literally "fucking around and finding out," as the kids say these days.

Six or so months later, I was pregnant.

People ask, "Were you trying?" Honestly, that's the dumbest fucking question. Yes, Brenda, he came inside of me. We know how it works.

What I wasn't prepared for was the mental mind-fuck it would be to watch and feel my body changing right before my eyes.

I mean, don't get me wrong, I had no issues being pregnant *(other than the fact that my cervix basically fell out of my vagina at sixteen weeks, I guess... more on that later)*. I never got sick or threw up, I didn't have any wild cravings for pickles dipped in peanut butter, and the only big food aversion I had was to the fresh basil in our garden that Brandon kept trying to sneak into literally every damn dish he cooked.

The roller-coaster of emotions you go through when you're pregnant is no joke. You're expected to be grateful and joyous at all times that there's a parasitic alien inside of you making you hate the way you look, but you're also somehow glowing and powerful at the same time.

I'm not sure I can fully put into words the mental shit show pregnancy was for me, but in an effort to get my feelings out, here's a journal entry I'd written:

*Deleted Scene: A Mother's Secret Journal Entry*

*I don't recognize myself in the mirror anymore. I know who I was, but I'm not sure who I am any more. This person is different. I don't look like me. This isn't me. My boobs are different. My legs are swollen. My face is tired. My eyes are empty. I can't even look into them. It's like looking into someone else's home, only they're not there, so it feels like spying.*

*I feel guilty for all of it. For feeling like an alien. For mourning my previous life.*

*I can't sit up on my own. I can't roll over. I can't sleep through the night. My favorite clothes don't fit. But no one cares. No one else is mourning the life of a girl trapped inside a body that's no longer familiar to her.*

*I'm ashamed to even have these thoughts. My depression runs on shame, pulling me deeper into the abyss of lost souls.*

*I want my daughter to be born into an environment of peace and love. I want her to feel nothing but loved. How can I give her that when all I feel is nothing?*

*That's not true. I feel confused. Guilty. Grateful. Ashamed. Happy. Lost. Excited. Sad. Hopeful. Heavy. Powerful. Different. Terrified.*

*I feel it all. I feel like a monster. So many out there pray for this. And here I am, with the audacity to release this deleted scene.*

*They don't show you this part. They cut it from every movie, skipping straight to the joy.*

*I can't be the only one. I can't be alone in this.*

*I've loved being pregnant. The little kicks. The tiny clothes. The sound of her heartbeat. Yet somewhere along the way I lost myself in the process.*

*It took so long to find myself the first time. To love me for me. To embrace all of my flaws. To step into my power unapologetically.*

*I'm working on my new identity. Peeling back layers and processing traumas I didn't know were deep inside. I'm figuring it out, how to love my body for the miracle it's creating.*

*I'm doing okay. I'm hanging in there. I'm still powerful. I'm still beautiful. I am loved. Worthy. And enough.*

*I am me, and I'm a MOM.*

HO-LY shit. Reading back through that journal entry brings tears to my eyes. Can you imagine the release I felt to get these thoughts out?

I'm not saying you need to go and write a short story every time something comes up for you, but I am recommending you find a way to recognize and process your emotions.

I hear you asking, *but how?*

How do you recognize what's going on inside of you? It's not always easy, but here's something you can try.

## The Feel-It-to-Heal-It Method

This framework for recognizing and releasing emotions came to me while writing this chapter, and I'm really fucking proud of it. Are you ready?

I invite you to take a deep breath in through your nose, holding it at the top for 3... 2... 1... and sigh it out through your mouth. Do it again, and really visualize the clean air entering your belly on your inhale, and the heaviness and whatever you need to release leaving your chest on your exhale. One last time, in through your nose, out through your mouth.

As you allow your breathing to return to normal, take a moment to do a mental scan of your body. Where are you feeling emotion? Where are you holding tension?

Are your shoulders tight? Is your chest heavy? Does your throat have a lump in it? *Really sink in and feel that.*

Once you've identified where this emotion is living in your body, let's examine further. Can you give it a name?

Is it anger?

Sadness?

Guilt?

Hurt?

Shame?

Fear?

...All of the above?

Try to narrow it down to the main, overarching emotion. Keep going deeper into the feeling until you feel like you're at the very beginning of it. Sometimes I like to process these out loud until the one thing really lands, and it's totally okay if you're not sure where that feeling is coming from; sometimes it doesn't even matter.

*"I'm feeling hurt."*

*"Something triggered this dread inside of me."*

*"I'm feeling guilty and ashamed, and I'm not sure why."*

*"I'm disappointed in myself about the way I acted this morning."*

*"I feel like my integrity has been questioned, and people don't trust me."*

As you process and begin to identify the root cause of this feeling, how can you give yourself love and release this?

Do you need to cry? Cool, do it.

Would you feel better if you apologized for something?

Want to get your journal out and write it all down?

Do you need to do some forgiveness work?

Talk to someone supportive to process?

Or was acknowledging it all you needed? Great. Bless and release that shit. You're done.

The feel-it-to-heal-it-method is simple: Recognize that you're feeling something, lean into it, identify it, and release it.

Remember what I said about the difference between simple and easy? Just because this method is simple, doesn't mean it's easy. Cut yourself some slack if this is new to you. Actually, cut yourself some slack if this isn't, too. In general, just cut yourself some fucking slack, okay?

Some emotions will come up and out much easier than others, and that's totally okay.

Some emotions will need longer to process.

Some have been inside for so long they basically moved in under the radar and are now claiming squatter's rights.

Listen, we're here on this Earth and living the human experience to FEEL ALL THE FEELS. We're here to lean into the discomfort and feel what's coming up so we can process and move through those things.

We're not dismissing emotional pain; we're making a conscious effort to recognize it.

If something absolutely devastating happens to you, what we're not going to do is "suck it up" and go about our lives while staying strong for everyone around us, and maybe we'll deal with it later when no one is watching, but, no, we end up just shoving it down forever and turning into the Grinch who stole Christmas or that scary animated monster house who eats children for breakfast because she's so lonely.

The main character in pretty much every single movie has a moment where they *feel and heal the big emotions that were causing conflict* (the Grinch when his heart grows three sizes), and that's exactly what the feel-it-to-heal-it-method is all about.

As you get more comfortable acknowledging and recognizing emotions when they come up, it will become easier for you to process and release them more quickly and smoothly so you can live a life unchained from trapped emotions.

I'm so grateful to this method because had I not processed the way I was feeling about my body during pregnancy, my daughter would have been born into an environment of body shame, negative self-talk, and sadness. Instead, she was born into a world where her mom knows she is a beautiful, loving, and powerful woman—stretch marks and all.

So my question to you, friend, is this:

What do you need to feel right now, so you can begin to heal?

*Now is the time, isn't it?*

## Feel It to Heal It Affirmation

*I lovingly allow myself to heal and move forward.*

## Feel It to Heal It Exercise

What do you need to feel to heal? Follow the framework in this chapter to help recognize and release emotions you've been holding on to.

# LET SHIT GO

*"Forgiveness is more than saying sorry."*

Raise your hand if you sang that in Anna Faris's voice from whatever movie that was with Ryan Reynolds.

(I Googled it: Just Friends.)

Lemme ask you, dear reader: When's the last time you forgave someone?

It's been a while, hasn't it?

Forgiveness can be tough because we think that if we forgive someone, it means what they did was okay. Or maybe it means we want them back in our lives. Or we have to keep putting up with their bullshit.

When in reality, forgiveness isn't for them. It's for you.

We forgive others so we can feel better, so we can release the negativity we're hanging on to, and so we can cut the energetic cords that were tying us together.

Not forgiving someone is like drinking poison and then expecting the other person to die. You're literally ingesting that negative energy and they're out there living their lives without a care. *(Woof, how many theirs, they'res, and theres can I cram into one sentence?)*

You ready for the really cool thing? Here it is: You can totally just _let shit go._

I highly recommend it, actually.

Because you choose what you give your energy to, remember?

I'm not saying that person didn't hurt you or that what happened to you was okay; what I am saying is you ultimately get to decide how long you want to hold onto that painful story.

There's this song on my Spotify favorites about forgiveness called _"My Healing"_ by Sophia Spallino—that I really don't even know how it came into my life but I'm obsessed with—and it's a beautiful mix of spoken word, drums, and harp that I 100% recommend you look up and listen to.

(Go do it. I'll wait.)

Beautiful, isn't it?

Forgiveness is about your healing.

You, the main character, deserve to feel free in your life. Free from the energetic cords of anger, sadness, fear, hurt, shame, guilt, and resentment. And it all starts with deciding to forgive.

Forgiving yourself.

Forgiving others.

Forgiving The Universe.

Forgiving in general.

In my opinion, forgiving yourself is one of the most powerful things you can do for your healing journey.

It's you taking radical responsibility for whatever it was that happened in your life, and by doing that, you're able to release yourself from the hold it has over you.

Any time I bring my shadows to light and acknowledge and forgive myself for them, I'm no longer ashamed of them. There's nothing anyone can say to me that I haven't already said to myself and worked through and forgiven myself for.

And if there is, I know exactly how to handle it.

Another really powerful song for letting shit go is *"You are Love"* by Lotus Sky. It features the Hawaiian forgiveness prayer, Ho'oponopono, which goes something like this: *"I love you, I'm sorry, please forgive me, thank you."* (*To learn more about this spiritual practice, Google "Ho'oponopono."*)

You know about forgiving others, but I'm curious, when was the last time you made a conscious decision to forgive *yourself?*

It took me many years, but I finally forgave myself for the things I did (and "failed" to do) and for so desperately seeking external love and validation when I didn't know who I was yet.

My past does not define me.

Because I know now that I am so much more than the choices I made in my past.

And so are you.

My coaching clients and I focus a lot on forgiveness work. *(Probably because I can't just tell them they need to let shit go and expect that to \*magic wand\* change their lives.)*

Forgiveness work is when you actively decide you're ready to feel different, so you go through some intentional practices designed to help you bring self-awareness to the issues and stories you've been clinging to. Through this release, you empower yourself, you reclaim your energy, and you are free.

I learned the following exercise during my coaching certification training. When I did it for the first time, I was overcome with emotion and have revisited this exercise many times. I share it here with permission, and added a bit to it, to pay it forward to you. Please use this as inspiration and feel free to do the exercise in the way that feels right to YOU.

*If you're reading this book and thinking about becoming a world-class coach, I got my certifications through six+ months of next-level intensive training and curriculum inside the Quantum Coaching Academy with Ashley Gordon and Jenna Teague. 10/10 recommend. Check it out at www.heymeganreed.com/QCA.*

## Forgiveness Exercise

Set the mood with a candle or a glass of wine/cup of tea. Ask Alexa to play: "You Are Love (Ho'oponopono)" by Lotus Sky on repeat on Spotify. Grab a journal, and set a timer for ten minutes. In this ten minutes, brain dump onto paper and/or aloud everyone and everything you need to forgive. I recommend you write it all out.

I forgive myself for _____.

I forgive my family for _____.

I forgive my parents for _____.

I forgive my friend for _____.

I forgive money for _____.

I forgive my body for _____.

I forgive the government for _____.

I forgive the whole world for _____.

And at the end of the time, I want you to go back through your list, read it out loud, reciting the Ho'oponopono prayer (*I love you, I'm sorry, please forgive me, thank you*) after each one... and then burn it.

The burning, for me, is a real symbolic and physical way of showing the Universe that I choose to release this pain both emotionally and spiritually. On all levels and forever.

And it really is emotional. For me, at least. To release something that once held so much weight/shame/guilt/dread/fear/anger?

I almost always cry.

Something else I like to do when I'm deep in the weeds of a situation that's bringing up a lot of emotions is to write a letter to the other person *with the distinct intention that they will never see it.* This healing is for your heart and your eyes only.

Truly, let it all out. Say what you need to say. The good, the bad, the ugly. Write the things you would never say out loud but you know you need to get off your chest. Cry about it. Rage about it. Yell about it. Stomp about it.

Feel it to heal it, remember?

And again, when you're done, BURN IT.

Like, really burn it. *Safely, of course.* Don't go burning your house down and then writing me a strongly worded letter saying this was my fault and I owe you a house and a million dollars for your trauma. You're a grown-ass adult. Use aluminum foil, have water nearby, whatever. *insert long-ass legal disclaimer here about fire safety and common sense*

When Brandon and I moved to Nashville—away from our friends and family—for a job he accepted after graduating chiropractic school, that was a really weird transition time for me. He'd been living there for almost six months before I left my dream job to join him, and when I got there, I felt completely lost and worthless. Having left what felt like my entire life behind, I had a loooooot of feelings swirling inside of me.

I resented the shit out of him, but I couldn't bring myself to say everything I was feeling for fear of severely damaging our relationship. *I'm also an Enneagram One, remember? So I tend to bottle up my anger.*

I was thinking some really mean shit. I woke up every day mad. And in our one-bedroom apartment, I did everything I could to avoid him, only I couldn't because I'd have to go through the bedroom to get to the closet and bathroom. Three pets and two humans in less than 600 square feet?

*Woof.*

*I was the one drinking the metaphorical poison and waiting around hoping he would die the slow painful death. Not really, but, also really.*

One night I was so fed up I poured a giant glass of red wine, locked the bedroom door, climbed into bed, and journaled for nearly an hour. I wrote everything out. Everything that was on my heart, and I ugly cried while doing it, knowing how much weight those feelings had on my chest.

And afterwards?

I felt so much better.

I forgave myself for the thoughts I was having. They were all valid and totally understandable. And I forgave Brandon for everything, too. Everything I was feeling was real, and to acknowledge it—rather than push it down forever or blow up and have a giant fight with Brandon and make things worse—was exactly what I needed.

Letting shit go can be a difficult process—I know—but it can also lead to emotional, physical, spiritual, and relational growth and healing. Remember, forgiveness is truly a personal process and may take time. It's totally okay if it does. It's important to work through the steps at your own pace, and release them in a way that feels right for you (even if it's rage journaling and ugly crying into a glass of wine).

It is safe to forgive.

## Let Shit Go Affirmation

*Forgiveness is a gift I choose to give myself.*

## Let Shit Go Exercises

1. Grab a journal, and set a timer for ten minutes. Brain dump everyone and everything you need to forgive. And at the end of the time, go back through your list, read it out loud, and then burn it.

2. Write a forgiveness letter. Leave nothing out. Cry about it. Burn it.

# YOUR SUPPORTING ROLES MATTER

Every main character has its circle of trusty friends, side-kicks, and secondary supporting characters.

- The ones who lift them up when things get weird. *(We love these.)*
- The ones who throw them under the bus for their own benefit. *(We don't love these.)*
- And the ones who are essentially loyal yet emotionally unavailable. *(Jury's still out.)*

The question is, who are yours?
*What kind of people are you allowing in your circle?*

The older I get, the more I believe quality over quantity is the way to go.

I would rather have three incredible friends with whom I can share anything and I know they'll still love me rather than thirteen mediocre friends who talk about me when I'm not around and make me feel small for being myself. Wouldn't you?

Harry Potter could have had literally any friends he wanted, but he cultivated two extremely high-quality friendships with Ron Weasley and Hermione Granger, didn't he?

The Smart People on the Internet say you're a combination of the five people you spend the most time with, so I want to invite you to take a second and evaluate your inner circle. Who are the five people you're giving the most energy and time to? (Mental energy counts. Bigtime.)

Do they give energy back?

Or do they only take it and drain the fuck outta you?

If they only take energy, it's time to find a new friend or lessen the amount of energy you're putting into that relationship for a while.

Because I don't know if anyone has told you this today, but you deserve to be surrounded by people who lift you up and make you feel like somebody who matters.

You deserve to be checked on, hyped up, seen, heard, celebrated, and treated like the magical creature you are.

Imagine how much different the Harry Potter story lines would have been if the annoying little twat, Draco Malfoy, was in Harry's inner circle.

*Real weird vibes, right?*

On that note, to have a tight-knit circle of quality friends, you must first *be* the kind of friend you're looking for, because friendship is a two-way street.

How does your ideal best friend act, and how can you embody those qualities in your current relationships?

As we get older, quality friendships may seem more difficult to make.

That's because we've got less time for the "dating" phase of friendship that we did back when we were in school. It takes intentional effort, so if you've got yourself someone in your life that you can rely on and that makes you a better person, let them know. And dedicate quality time with them. Water that friendship garden.

Not that you asked—I mean, you kinda did, since you're reading this book—but here's my recipe for a successful friendship.

## Recipe For a Successful Friendship

**Work on your self-awareness.**

The more you know and understand yourself, the easier it will be to identify traits in a friend that align with yours. You'll also be more comfortable showing up as your true self, which in turn, will invite others to do the same. In my experience, when you find friends who are also working on their shit, the drama levels stay down, the conversations are deeper, and the connections are stronger.

*(This is something we focus heavily on inside the Creating Confidence® Society. We've created a safe and empowering space for members to dive deep, show up authentically, and learn more about themselves and who they are with the support of others on a similar journey. I'll include a link in the resources section in the*

*back of the book, and also here it is right now in case you're feeling called to join us inside:* heymeganreed.com/society.*)*

**Assume good intentions, always.**

Before having my daughter, I used to be a really good tex-ter. Like, I almost always responded or got back to you that same day. Usually within the hour.

Nowadays, you never know what you're going to get from me.

If I'm working or on a coaching call, I either don't have my phone near me at all, I have it turned off, or I'll see it pop up, dismiss it, and then forget to come back to it. If I'm "mom-ing" (a verb I really love), I do my best to stay present, so if I happen to open your text and don't mark it unread—a really cool new feature, praise the Lord for it—I will literally not text you back for days or weeks or some-times never. If there's a request or question that requires actual thinking, scheduling, or checking my calendar, it will sit unread until I have the energetic capacity to dive in.

My intentions with all of these are good. My friends know this.

At least, I hope they do, and I extend them the same lee-way. I'm not over here wondering why they didn't text me back and maybe they're mad at me and we're not friends anymore. I always assume positive intent unless given a le-git reason to believe otherwise.

**Be open and curious.**

Ask questions, and listen. Truly listen.

That means listen without thinking about what you're going to say next or what you're gonna eat in half an hour.

Listen without judgment.

Ask your inner circle things like: *How's work going? How's your heart? What do you need? How can I support you with that?*

**Say what you feel.**

If something is going well and you're really vibing, awesome. Tell them you appreciate their friendship.

On the other hand, if you're feeling like you need to apologize for something, share your feelings, or set a boundary, do it. You cannot expect anyone to read your mind—not even your best friends or your partner—so it's better to get something off your chest than to shove it down, let it simmer, and potentially burn the relationship when it boils up later.

Honesty is always the best policy.

I'm still working on this, but I find the more open and real we can be with each other, the stronger our bonds can grow.

**Embrace your differences.**

No two people in this world are alike. That's so fucking cool, isn't it? You are unique AF. Which means, while you and your friends may have quite a bit in common, there's going to be things you disagree on. True friendship is a mutual love and respect for your differences. (Because you know they have good intentions, right?)

Maybe your best friend went to the Taylor Swift Eras Tour but the idea of being surrounded by that many people makes you anxious as hell so you stayed home. That's cool, you can still be friends.

Maybe your friend is a vegan but you eat greasy cheese-burgers like it's your middle name. That's cool, you can still be friends.

Maybe your best friend got all the COVID-19 shots and boosters and you made an informed decision not to. That's cool, you can still be friends.

You can still be friends ... *if you want.*

Friendship is a choice. A partnership. An agreement. It's you deciding to say, "I see you for YOU, and I love you because of that."

### Don't gossip, ever.

This one is difficult, but crucial. If someone shares private information with you, that's between you and them. When I started keeping secrets safe and eliminating gossip, the level of trust in my relationships rose, and now my friends feel like they can confide in me with anything. (*Also, if you tell me a secret these days, odds are pretty fucking good I'm gonna forget about it LOL.*) Sometimes I do slip, though, and when I do, I feel pretty shitty about it because it's out of integrity with my values. I recognize it, apologize, forgive myself, and move forward.

I also make an effort not to say anything about my friends that I wouldn't want them to hear that I said from someone else, because that feels shitty and breaks trust. The Golden Rule, right? I'm attracting people into my circle who don't have the capacity in their cups for any low-vibe, energy-draining tasks like gossiping.

Your supporting roles make a huge difference in your Main Character experience, so take a moment to evaluate who you've cast in your story and the roles they're playing in your life.

And remember that to them, you're THEIR supporting role.

Kind of a mind fuck, isn't it?

*We are all supporting characters.*
*And we are all main characters.*

## Your Supporting Roles Matter Affirmation

*I surround myself with empowering people who make me feel good about myself.*

## Your Supporting Roles Matter Exercises

1.   Who are the five people you spend the most time with? List 'em. For each:
     a) Do they give or take energy? Or both, in a balanced way overall?
     b) Evaluate where you can make adjustments if needed. For example, talk to them about it, adjust how much you give, or move them from inner circle to another rung out, etc. *This applies to family, too.*

2.   How can you be the kind of friend you'd like to have?
     a) How does this friend act? What do they do?
     b) Make a plan to do those things.

# IF YOUR HEART LEAVES, TAKE YOUR BODY WITH IT

This chapter is about living life in alignment with your values.

This chapter is also about a time when I wasn't.

When I left what I'd thought was my dream job designing greeting cards in Kansas City to move to Nashville to live with my husband *(wait... you don't know this whole story yet, do you)?*

Let me back up and give you a quick little recap.

Brandon and I got married while he was still in chiropractic school. I worked full time at a big name card company and I fucking loved it. Before he graduated, he accepted a three-month preceptorship (fancy medical-world term for unpaid internship) in Nashville, Tennessee, working for probably the most genuine human on the planet. *(Hi, Audra!)* We sold our house, moved him to Nashville at the end of September, and I moved in with his parents so I could keep my job and pay for Brandon's $1700/month one-bedroom apartment in East Nashville.

The plan was for Brandon to complete his preceptorship, graduate, and then I would move to Nashville as well. I had worked out a sweet deal with my current directors at the time *(who were also amazing–I love you, Ashlee and Mandy!)* so that when I eventually did move—we didn't really even set a timeline on it—I would be able to keep my job and continue designing cards remotely from Nashville. They completely trusted me to get my work done, and we had been testing remote working together as I flew back and forth visiting Brandon.

It was truly the best of both worlds. I got to travel and work from wherever I was while doing what I loved. *I was getting a taste of that entrepreneurship freedom I didn't know I was craving.*

Fast forward a few months of airport travel and living with my in-laws, and the card company went through a giant reorganization. I was scheduled to be moved to the Christmas-card team under a new boss.

To be fair, this new boss didn't know me at all, but when I told her about my situation and my plans to move soon, she communicated her discomfort and took it up the leadership chain.

I was crushed. If you know anything about large corporations, once something goes up the leadership chain, you can pretty much be sure you're fucked. All it takes is for one person to disagree, and it's all over.

My place at the company was in limbo for weeks.

No matter how many people at the company had my back and knew how hard I worked *(and, to 100% toot my own horn, how good I was at it)*, it didn't matter.

A meeting notification popped up on my calendar for a Friday afternoon with my current art director and editorial director (never a good sign) and in a tiny-ass planning room, they told me I had a job at the company... for as long as I lived locally.

We all sat there and cried. Which sounds ridiculous now, but for everything we had worked towards to come crashing down in an unfortunate turn of events outside of our control was truly heartbreaking.

I had to choose between my husband and my dream job.

We all knew I couldn't stay. I had been living apart from Brandon for months, and I had already begun making plans to move mid-March.

I negotiated terms so I could stay until the end of February to wrap up the cards I'd been designing as part of Ashlee and Mandy's team until I left *(because I wasn't about to do ANY work for the Christmas art director)*.

They agreed we could make that work, and threw me a going-away party that only a card company in the business of relationship-building could throw—we're talking artfully-decorated cakes, balloons, flower arrangements, hand-lettered farewell cards, hugs, and heartfelt speeches.

On my last day, after I had loaded my car with all of my cubicle decor, my entire team rolled me and my office chair down the elevator and out through the mile-long concrete hallway as we cried and they sang the saddest farewell song imaginable (that I can't quote for you because of copyright bullshit).

I remember sitting in my car in the parking garage crying until I burst a blood vessel in my right eye and then continuing to cry the entire way home while blasting Sia in my speakers.

This job was my identity.

Who was I if I wasn't a designer at one of the most well-known greeting card companies in the world?

The next day, I loaded up the car with our dog, all my shit, a handful of snacks, and headed for Tennessee.

After a couple months of mentally struggling, reading personal-development books, going to networking events trying to make friends, and freelance designing for some friends back in Kansas, I decided it was time to leave the apartment. I needed a job that required me to interact with humans again.

I joined one of those talent-sourcing head-hunting companies, and landed an interview within two days at a big-name financial company in Brentwood, Tennessee.

It was an easy win for me.

They'd been interviewing for weeks, and my portfolio and history designing cards were impressive. I'd done the debt-free thing, so I understood the lingo of the company and knew of the man behind their mission.

It all fell into place perfectly, and I started contract-designing printed marketing materials there the following week. I was so excited to be part of something big and ready to help humans on a large scale again.

As you can probably tell, by the title of this chapter, this is the part of the story where things fell out of alignment.

Now, I grew up in the Methodist church, but I always felt this weird disconnect with the way religion was forced on me as a child when I literally didn't even know who I was, let alone some higher power and my relationship with them.

So on my second day, when I met with the head of HR for onboarding and he asked me if I'd found a church yet, I lied and said, "Yeah, totally. My husband and I love the Crosspoint church by our apartment in East Nashville."

I was caught off guard. *First of all, are you even allowed to ask me that? You're the fucking head of human resources,* I remember thinking.

That was the first red flag: the fact that I had to lie about my religious beliefs to fit in.

Weeks went by, and I grew close to most of the people on my team and surrounding teams. I got to be part of the move to their new building south of Franklin, and they constantly were dropping comments about me joining full time.

Little did they know, I was flying under the radar at this company. Not only did I have a secret credit card *(gasp!)*, I believed that women deserved the same rights as men *(double gasp!)*, and I didn't agree with the way people mocked our two Puerto Rican team members. But if you had a different opinion on something, you were verbally ridiculed or dismissed, so I stayed silent and let my disbelief and sense of outraged indignation fester.

As a contract worker, I wasn't allowed to attend company-wide functions *(I couldn't even be on the property during the Wednesday morning devotional)*, and with the drive being almost forty-five minutes both ways, I kept pushing for them to let me remote work because I didn't want to be in the office. *(How many red flags are we up to now?)*

Surely I wasn't the only one hiding out of fear of being ostracized.

Four months into my six-month contract that the company was planning to extend, the biggest red flag I'd ever experienced in a corporate workplace happened. Please enjoy this journal entry I wrote to process the anger I had felt after being sexually harassed by my project manager:

> *Have you ever stood up for yourself?*

> *Maybe you waited a while—because the pain and discomfort were too fresh. Or maybe you played it off originally as a joke, and then didn't feel validated in your desire to say something because you downplayed it upfront.*

> *My creative leader today asked me in an informal exit interview about my experience at the company. And while there was an intense hesitation, I was eventually honest.*

> *Honest about my excitement to leave and never look back. Honest about the racism, sexism, and bigotry I'd witnessed. Honest about the sexual harassment I'd directly been through.*

> *And now I'm being honest with you.*

*Two months ago, in a private meeting room dis-cussing missed budgets and bar-graph projections with three adult men—my direct leaders—my body was verbally objectified by one of the men, and my discomfort was mocked repeatedly. Less than an hour later, there was an email in my inbox from the same man, to all four of us from the meeting, with my face hack-job edited onto a movie poster with the altered words: "The Girl with the Back Tattoo."*

*I was uncomfortable. I reply-all'd with "lolol never seen it" and forwarded it to two of my friends on the team in disbelief. The other two men, leaders over the harasser, said nothing.*

*What this man doesn't know is I've been harassed before. I've been assaulted before. So a few "jokes" and discomfort about my body are a pretty easy thing to sweep under the rug, relatively speaking.*

*But what he didn't think about is the mental place that kind of discomfort can trigger someone back into.*

*What he also doesn't know is how it felt when I kept my sexual assault to myself for years, or that I couldn't stand up for myself, because I'd never done it.*

*Today, I stood up.*

*But I didn't do it for me. I did it for the new girl, who used to be a Dallas Cowboys cheerleader. I stood up for the person who fills the marketing designer position after me. For the admin assistant who I adore. For the females of the company, and the women of the world.*

*What he doesn't know is that I stood up.*

*And this time, I'm not sitting down.*

I didn't quit right away. In fact, I tried to play it off like it wasn't a big deal. But it haunted me to be surrounded by people who: a) didn't know who I was, and b) didn't give a shit about me, either.

I used to have that picture saved on my computer. The one that—let's just call him Paul—emailed out to me and his managers, Bill and Chris, with my face Photoshopped on a movie poster. But every time I saw it, it took me back to a place I didn't like going, so I deleted it.

Not long after this happened, I was allowed the gracious treat of attending one of their all-company meetings where the guest speaker, an ex-Navy Seal, was talking about his time in the service and his dedication to the Lord. I only remember one thing from his presentation, and it was this: *"If your heart leaves, take your body with it."*

I knew my heart had left the company. I didn't want to be there. I would disappear from my cubicle to work on my own shit in a private room. I had been taking notes in every meeting on how I could apply these strategies to my own business. I had been living out of alignment with my values for months, and it was slowly eating away at my soul. I'd never experienced such a strange work environment that fostered religious and racial discrimination and operated like a secret cult, especially after coming from a company that had made such an effort to cultivate a culture of inclusion. I remember telling Brandon I was going to write a book about my time there and call it *Racism, Sexism, and Bigotry: Doing the Lord's Work.*

Thanks, Navy Seal guy.
Your talk was so inspirational that I left.

I'm grateful for this journey, nevertheless, because it led me to this moment right now, where I'm following my dreams and making an impact in the world on my own.

There's truly a silver lining in everything.

It took me a while to see it, especially after leaving what was my then dream job, but had I never been forced to do something else, I might still be designing cards. And while I really enjoyed the creative work with cards, it isn't the highest use of my skills and the deepest devotion of my heart and soul. Because had I never followed my heart right out the door of a company that didn't align with my values, I would have never started my coaching business—one that's helped hundreds of people get to know and love who they truly are.

*Trust that your heart knows what it's doing.*

Psst—Bet you're wondering what happened to "Paul" after I spilled the tea in my exit interview, aren't you? *He still fucking works there.* Insider tea has it that he was demoted and moved to another team for a while.

## If Your Heart Leaves, Take Your Body with It Affirmation

*I stand up for what I believe in.*


## If Your Heart Leaves, Take Your Body with It Exercise

1.   Where is your heart? Evaluate the things you dream about and care most about.

2.   What actions can you begin to take this week to help move your body closer to where your heart is?

# FAILURE IS A BLESSING

*\*\*\*My advanced readers suggested I add a trigger warning here for you. This chapter shares my story of self-harm, depression, and suicide attempts. Please skip the first part of this chapter if you need to for your mental health. **I've indicated where the story ends with three big asterisks.***

The first time I tried to take my own life, I failed.

As a Type A perfectionist, and at the time an unidentified Enneagram One, I was a blatant rule follower. So when the Tylenol bottle said not to exceed eight capsules in twenty-four hours, I took ten... and waited to die.

I had been harming myself for a year before that. Trying to feel the same pain on the outside that I felt on the inside. Scratching the surface of my skin with sharp fingernails until I bled. But carefully, so I could hide it from my family.

My mom saw once. "Where did you learn how to do this?" she asked. And when I didn't answer her, we never talked about it again.

It was a fall day in my freshman year of high school when I took the pills. I remember crying a few hours later with uncertainty. My bones felt strange. My skin was buzzing, and my mouth had a sour, chemical taste in it. If I breathed in really deep, I could smell the Tylenol permeating my body.

By the end of the day, my body was so numb that nothing hurt, and I went to volleyball practice like usual. I noticed diving for serves didn't hurt, and I had fun throwing myself at the ground.

Nothing happened that day.

The second time I tried, I wasn't messing around. Sixteen pills, that should do it. That's double the maximum recommended amount. I spent the day withdrawn and sad, sort of mentally saying goodbye to everything but relieved for it all to be over.

I could smell the Tylenol in my body. A distinct, acrid smell you never forget. I could taste the chemicals in my mouth. The only thing I could feel was my heart racing.

And still nothing happened.

I was running out of pills. And the big capsules were hard to take. Did you know they make small, round, red Tylenol coated in a sweet flavoring for easier swallowing?

I sat alone on the bench in the girls' locker room before school. A high-school freshman, just before spring break. I'd just spent an entire school year of my life wishing I didn't exist. I don't even remember my teachers from that year. It was all a blur.

I had twenty-two pills counted out. Or was it thirty-three? I can't remember now.

I peeled the label off nervously.

Someone walked in while I was taking them. Ignoring In-visible Me, she grabbed her bag and left as quickly as she came.

Pills gone, I tossed the bottle, left the locker room, and went to class.

It was pi day. March 14. (*3.14, get it?*) Our PE class was taking a field trip to play frisbee golf. On the bus on the way to the course, I sat next to a boy named Jake. He was a nice guy—a friend—and I asked him if he'd ever taken so much Tylenol he could smell it. He looked uncomfortable and worried.

It was a really strong smell. I remember weird details from the trip. The grass was still wet from the early-morn-ing dew and my light-wash flared jeans and shoes got all wet. I think I slept on the way back.

I woke up on the gym floor, alone. How did I get there? What class was I supposed to be in? Where was everyone? My stomach hurt. I couldn't see straight. I pulled myself up from the hardwood floor where the bleachers go when they fold out, stumbled to the locker room, and grabbed the label-less, empty bottle of pills from the trash.

Next thing I know, I'm in the counselor's office, handing her the empty bottle and crying silently.

Her face went white. She asked questions. "How many did you take? How long ago?" She made phone calls.

"I don't feel good," I said.

My parents picked me up and took me to the emergency room. It was too late to pump my stomach, and with the bottle being empty, they couldn't know for sure what I ingested, so they couldn't use activated charcoal.

I was on my own.

I could hear my parents talking to the doctors in hushed tones outside my hospital room as I lay there sick and numb. A social worker came in. I answered questions. I threw up. It burned. My mom held the pan but wouldn't look at me. I never saw my dad.

They transported me to a mental-health facility. I was a danger to myself. A cop car pulled up to the ER in the kind of car with the bars on the windows. Two large women with thick accents and short, buzzed hair were up front. They made small talk the whole way, and I watched silently out the back window as my parents' vehicle on the interstate slipped farther and farther out of sight.

\* \* \*

I tell my clients there's no such thing as failure—only valuable lessons. *"What learnings can you take away from this experience?"* I ask.

Because failure isn't real. It doesn't exist. At least, in my world it doesn't.

I didn't FAIL at suicide.

I mean, logistically, I totally did. The odds were 50/50, and I both won AND lost at the same time.

I didn't FAIL, because I learned some very valuable lessons. While I couldn't see them at the time, I'm just now—as a grown-ass adult—connecting the dots that maybe I'm here on this Earth for a greater purpose.

*And unless you simply never try, there is no way you can fail.*

The literal only way for this book to fail is for me to never even work on it. Anything else is a lesson to be learned.

If I don't publish it?
*A lesson that it didn't truly matter to me.*

If I don't tell the world I wrote a book?
*A lesson about hiding.*

If I don't sell any books?
*LOL, not gonna happen. Thanks for being here.*

Mistakes are important.

Without them, we never learn, grow, or gain the ever-elusive *clarity* we're all searching for. Hate to break it to you, but clarity is built through action, Buck-o.

If you never try, you'll never know.

*And if you never know, then what's the fucking point?*

If you're ever in a moment where you're feeling like you've "failed," first, I want you to acknowledge your heartache.

Remember *Feeling It to Heal It?* What we're not doing is shoving everything down real deep.

It's totally understandable that you would be grieving an expectation that didn't see itself into fruition.

You were looking forward to it.

You'd dreamed about it.

You had it all planned out.

Of course you're in your feels because it didn't work out like you'd hoped.

This feeling is part of the human experience.

But let me ask you something here....

WHAT IF everything had worked out exactly as it was supposed to?

WHAT IF you'd bought that new house and then hated it because it led you to your dream house?

What if you didn't get that job or promotion or that romantic partner because the Universe had something better for you?

What if you didn't sign that new client because they would have been the world's worst client ever?

What if no one enrolled in your group coaching program because you didn't really want to run it anymore or you were already burning/burnt out?

While you may not have been able to see it at the time, failure is a blessing.

Failure gives you answers.
Answers bring you clarity.
Clarity brings you motivation.
Motivation brings you confidence.

And confidence brings you here.

## Failure Is a Blessing Affirmation

*I embrace failure as a stepping stone towards what's meant for me.*

## Failure Is a Blessing Exercises

1. List out five times in life that you "failed."

2. Now, address each one with curiosity. What lesson can you take away from this experience? *(Make it positive and empowering. None of that "I suck at X, Y, and Z bullshit.)*

3. Next time you "feel like a failure," feel the feels, acknowledge your disappointment, and when you're ready, embrace the lesson, and give yourself gratitude and grace.

# YOU ARE WORTHY JUST AS YOU ARE

This lesson's really important:

You are worthy, just as you are. You are worthy, just as you are. You are worthy, just as you are. You are worthy, just as you are. You are worthy, just as you are. You are worthy, just as you are. You are worthy, just as you are.

*You are worthy, just as you are.*

## You Are Worthy Just As You Are Affirmation

*I am worthy, just as I am.*

## You Are Worthy Just As You Are Exercise

The next time your Inner Critic pipes up, come back and read this chapter. Say it, write it, read it, feel it.

# YOUR STORY NEEDS YOU

Do you prioritize your mental health?

I like to think I do, but when I'm in the thick of it, it sure feels like it doesn't fucking matter.

It's difficult to remember moments of joy when you're struggling, isn't it?

All I can say is hang in there.

Get out of the house. Go for a walk. Shower. Get dressed. Exercise. Drink water. Practice affirmations. Soak up some sun. Call a friend. Tap it out. Journal. Have a snack. Drink some tea. Cry. Get a massage. Take a bath. Do yoga. Throw ice cubes. Make shitty art.

Do whatever makes you feel even a little bit better.

Whatever brings you a little bit back to yourself.

*Because you are loved, you matter, and you are enough.*

Here's something that's both liberating and terrifying at the same time: Not only are you the main character of your story, you're also the author.

So you get to decide—for the most part—what happens.

This, right here, is my plea to you and the writer of every show we've ever watched and loved *(I'm looking at you,*

*Shonda Rhimes, and what happened to Derek Shepherd in* Grey's Anatomy*)*:

Don't kill off the main character.

You are the main character for a reason. Your story literally needs you.

*You know this, don't you?*

I spent a lot of time struggling with my story.

Who was I?

Why was I here?

Who even cares?

A decade after surviving a massive suicide attempt, I was in my feels about it and wrote the following in an effort to heal what I was struggling to process. I'm going to warn you now, it's raw.

But it's important.

> *I remember the day the lights went out like it was yesterday. The 10-year anniversary came and went, raining feelings of anxious guilt and leaving behind a cloud of disappointed self-reflection.*

> *This is all I've become since then? I've changed a lot, but I am the same.*

> *Speak up, speak my mind, stay quiet. I live with my thoughts. I hide them behind a mask of humor and sarcasm. I'm funny. Really, I am. I crush it. I'm fine.*

*I watch my friends do life. They've started blogs and businesses and live behind the happy filter of social media and the pressure to showcase their flawless lives. No one is real.*

*I bought a house. I'm paying off debts and cutting up credit cards and doing taxes and being married, and somewhere along the path to adulthood I forgot where I left myself.*

*Somewhere ten years ago, probably.*

*Ten years ago, I was fifteen. I was lost, a child wandering the depths of her darkest fears. Drowning under the weight of never being good enough. Pretty enough. Smart enough. Athletic enough.*

*Enough.*

*Does anyone ever feel like they are enough? Is that a thing I should be able to feel? Middle-child syndrome, lost in between two sisters who never did anything wrong. Family disappointment, the one with the tattoos. Sorry, Mom.*

*Sorry.*

*I can feel sorry. An overwhelming, overtaking ocean of sorry. I feel sorry really well. Sorry so strong that it ruins my entire day. Guilt, anxiety, and overthinking. My specialty.*

*I have a few specialties. A ton, actually. I can't settle on just one, though. I don't know who I am, remem-*

*ber? To commit to a specialty might make me have to decide. Am I afraid of myself?*

*What am I? I'm a writer, maker, artist, designer. All of those. But none of them.*

*Who am I? I'm a wife. To a husband who can't understand, can't wrap his head around what I'm feeling. Who gets upset with me for living in my head, hiding under the covers in broad daylight. Who feels frustrated and helpless because he can't help me.*

*But he tries. I'm trying, too.*

*Trying to find myself. I cut my hair. I still don't know who I am. Less myself, maybe. I'm still lost. Ten years of soul-searching and the results are inconclusive. Why am I here, wasting the second chance I was given? Why, ten years later, am I the same fucking person?*

*I still need approval. Lost in a desire to belong, I need praise. I don't like going to parties because a crowd full of people is where I feel the most invisible. I need someone to remind me that I'm okay, and I'm not alone. I can't remember it all on my own. Sympathize with me. Someone validate me, please.*

*Please.*

*I'm a high performer at work. I know this about myself, it's not a secret. Yet my year-end review put me in the "average" category. The political corporate world* shared a laugh over my self-esteem and crushed it without looking back.

I'm fine.

My life is perfect. The American Dream, or whatever. Complete with mental instability and a recent diagnosis of Crohn's Disease, I am really crushing it.

Don't get me wrong. Amidst all this insecurity and bitterness, I am able to find plenty of joy. I love food. I enjoy going outside and riding my bike and playing with my cats. I'm an aunt, and it is so amazing. But I'm also trapped. Trapped inside a curtained room of emotions leftover from my past that only allow me a window of sunshine every now and then when the clouds decide it's okay to part.

When do you know who you are? Do you ever? Am I the only one stumbling through life, searching for their purpose?

The tenth anniversary of living came and went, and nobody said anything.

"Congrats on living! We're so happy you're here."

Maybe they forgot.

I remember the day the lights went out. And I am searching, hoping, and waiting for them to come back on.

Sometimes I think about the fact that I shouldn't still be here, yet here I am.

And I can't help but think that it's for a reason, you know?

In the summer of 2017, I was in a car accident with my best friend, Kelsey.

Her boyfriend and his friend were driving us home after a Thursday night concert in downtown Kansas City. On the way, we were sideswiped by a vehicle changing lanes.

I still remember little details like it was yesterday. It was dark out, probably 10:30 p.m. The speed limit was 65 miles per hour, and I was on the phone in the backseat with Kelsey in the seat next to me. I caught a flash of light, had time to say, "What the fuck!?" Then a deafening crunch sent the SUV spinning and my phone flying. Every side of our vehicle hit the concrete barrier as we spun out of control. The windows shattered, and when the car finally came to a stop, it was totaled.

Somewhere in the screaming, I bit my tongue so hard it was swollen and bleeding.

Ambulances came.

We were in shock.

It was one of the most terrifying events of our lives, and while we're both still processing the trauma of the experience even today, one thing we know for sure: We're lucky as fuck we survived.

Everything that night—other than the accident, obviously—went our way.

The concrete barrier didn't break, which saved us from a fifteen-foot free fall.

Kelsey and I had been drinking, so we stayed loose during the impact.

We didn't even have our seat belts on—we'd had the seats down from loading up her trunk earlier that day, and when we couldn't find them in the dark parking garage, we drunkenly opted to do without and yet somehow managed to stay inside the vehicle during the crash.

Looking back, there's absolutely no denying that everything happens for a reason.

There's just some reason we're supposed to be here, you know?

A reason that maybe I don't understand and never will, but I know for a fact that I'm going to spend the rest of my life making it worth it.

And the same goes for you.

You've been through some shit in your life that maybe you shouldn't have made it through, but you did, because you're here for a reason. Whatever that reason is, whether you understand it, comprehend it, or can see it or not, it's real.

So take care of yourself.
Prioritize your mental health.
And wear your seat belt.

Your story needs you.

*Congrats on living! I'm so happy you're here.*

## Your Story Needs You Affirmation

*I am here for a reason, whether I know it right now or not.*

## Your Story Needs You Exercises

1. How can you prioritize your mental health? Brain dump a list of activities that make you feel a little better, and reference it when you need a boost.

2. Reflect: What are you here for?

# YOU CAN DO HARD THINGS

It's 6 o'clock on the morning after my daughter turned seven months, and I'm sitting here pumping what I like to call boob juice (to make the fact that a machine is sucking my nipples into raspberries more enjoyable), and I'm wondering *how the fuck am I ever going to finish my book with a baby?*

We finally get her down for bed in the evenings, and the last fucking thing I want to do is work or clean. What I really want to do is watch the new season of *The Handmaid's Tale* or go to bed at 8 p.m., but then when would I get anything done?

I get it now.
Why parents are so tired.
This is fucking hard.

In the past, when my coaching clients with children would say, "I just don't have time or energy," I would question them every time. "Do you really not have time, or do you not have clear priorities?"

I don't say that anymore.

Like, now I feel pretty good about their priorities being clear. A totally vulnerable brand-new human being is the highest priority one can ever fucking have.

They just don't have the capacity right now, and that's totally understandable. I know for a fact how difficult it is to want to be a present mom *and* want to be making ninja business moves at the same time. This shit ain't for the faint of heart, and it's a daily power struggle between the feminine and masculine energies.

As I reflect on all of the difficult things I've done in life for this chapter, I'm immediately taken back to hands down THE most difficult of them all: Sonora's birth. Her natural, unmedicated birth. *insert that little emoji face here with the eyes that are spinning all dizzy-like*

I still can't believe I did that.

**It all started at 4:39 p.m. on Wednesday, March 16, 2022.**

I'm lying in bed browsing TikTok and pouting. *I really thought I'd have had my baby by now.* The doctors *all* thought I would deliver early, and hell, here I am two days from her due date and still fucking pregnant.

Lemme rewind and catch you up real quick.

When I was sixteen weeks pregnant I went pee—like any regular human does—but when I wiped, something was hanging out of me. I panicked, grabbed the mirror from under the sink, and inspected the situation. There, hanging out at the entrance of my vagina was what looked like a cer-

vix. I was terrified. Hours later, after some serious ugly crying and an ER visit, it was confirmed I had a third-degree
cervical prolapse. They placed a pessary (a donut-shaped
device shoved up there in an effort to keep the goods inside), and I was to be on pelvic rest for the remainder of my
pregnancy. No lifting anything over twenty lbs, no running,
no squatting, no coughing, no sex.

The goal was to keep the baby inside for as long as possible. What should have been an exciting and celebratory time
was laced with fear, and we kept the news of our pregnancy
quiet from the outside world until we felt ready. We didn't
know how to share such good, happy news when we were so
anxious and uncertain. Each week was a milestone.

So I was pouting. Because when they took the pessary
out after a weird early-labor scare at thirty-five weeks, my
doctors and doulas wanted me to be prepared to go into labor at any time, and very quickly because my cervix was
already labor-soft.

Four long-ass weeks later, I heard and felt something pop
in my pelvis. I said a casual "what the fuck" out loud, and
then made a dash for the toilet. My water had broken.

I called Brandon, who had conveniently ridden his bike to
his office to record a podcast episode, blurted out that my
water just broke, and suggested that maybe he get a ride
home AfuckingSAP.

I then called my doula, Jessica, who recommended I take a
hot shower, put on a disposable diaper, and keep her posted.

**7:30 p.m. Wednesday, March 16.**

This is where it all started to get a little fuzzy. The contractions had begun, and we were doing our best to ignore them for as long as possible. We ate an early dinner, watched that new *Turning Red* panda movie on Disney+, I sat on the bouncy ball in the shower, and finally decided to try and get some sleep.

^^All while the contractions were gradually intensifying. I could barely watch the movie, the shower didn't help, and we didn't have a fucking bathtub. The electrical stimulation (TENS) machine didn't do anything for me, either, and there was zero sleeping to be had.

Brandon didn't have much trouble tracking my contractions because I was pretty vocal about them. It was Moan City. I swear our pets thought I was either dying or calling in some ancient spirits.

**2:00 a.m. Thursday, March 17.**

My body felt like it was already pushing the baby out. The contractions were intense, yet still a little inconsistent, so it was hard to tell when it was time to leave for the birth center.

Brandon sent Jessica a video of one of my contractions, gave her the tracking and timing details, and we were instructed to meet her at the birthing center.

The car contractions were shitty. I had four in the fifteen minutes it took us to get there, and then a few more in the parking lot before making it inside.

I'm gonna be real with you, I was screaming at this point. *And in the middle of Corporate Woods in Overland Park, Kansas.*

We got inside where my OB performed a cervical check and informed me I was only dilated to one or two centimeters.

I felt the blood drain out of my face.

*...What? Are you kidding me?*

I knew it was a possibility, but I was devastated. They wouldn't admit me to a room and said I could either go back home or hang out and walk the halls until they could do another cervical check and I was farther along. Completely unwilling to get back in the car, I labored around the birthing center for what felt like an eternity

**4:00 or 5:00 a.m. Thursday, March 17.**

I'd been moaning around the halls of the birthing center long enough that my OB was ready to check me again. Desperate to not be spread-eagle on the table during a contraction, we did the world's fastest check and determined I was dilated to a four or a five.

*Sweet success.* I got into a room and the on-call midwife began filling the birthing tub with warm water.

I labored in the tub for what felt like another forever. *How many eternities of pain can a girl take?* Brandon put on the spiritual birth playlist I had created early in my third trimester and pulled up a seat right next to the tub. The warm water felt nice, but no position was comfortable. I spent most of my time in the tub on all fours begging the baby to come out already.

Like I said, things are a little fuzzy at this point looking back. During the contractions, I couldn't think of anything but the intensity. I basically blacked out. In between—which was never very long—I only had the time and energy to mutter one-word sentences like "water" or "tea." (Jessica had made me a cup of throat coat tea because of all the guttural screaming.)

Brandon says I was funny and singing in between contractions and everyone enjoyed me but one of the only things I remember saying was "shit, that's fresh" when I took a sip of tea. The rest is a blur.

I was allowed to have any food I wanted, but only ever had time for Brandon to feed me slurps of an applesauce pouch in between contractions.

The nurses would periodically come in and take my temperature or check the baby's heart rate but for the most part, Brandon and I were left alone in our room. Looking back, I'm grateful that I wasn't hooked up to any monitors or stuck with any needles.

Things started to feel real AF when I put my hand down to see if I could feel her head at all—and I got a handful of hair. Actual fucking HAIR. On. My. Baby's. Head.

I remember feeling amazed and saying to Brandon, "I think she has hair!"

Oh yeah, and somewhere in there during a contraction I pooped in the tub, and Brandon got to fish it out with a little net. *Isn't he just the best?*

**7:53 a.m. Thursday, March 17.**

I could feel her head stretching the shit out of me at this point. I'd been pushing for a little while in the water, blood and fluid floating all around.

A nurse came in and whispered something to my doula, who replied: "Are you fucking kidding me?"

I was then notified that they didn't have a second midwife on staff until 8 a.m. so I would have to get out of the tub.

Another nurse asked, "What if the midwife is early?"

To which the first replied, "What if she's not?"

What felt like ten people came into the room to help me climb out of the tub *while crowning.* (Literally the worst fucking timing.) Multiple towels dried off my limbs and body as I climbed onto the king-sized bed. I had a contraction so quickly that I stayed on all fours to push for a while.

I could barely hold myself up, I was so tired. I tried switching positions to a side-lying position with Brandon holding my leg but I had next to no energy or power in that position. After a few contractions, back to all fours I went.

At some point near the end I remember hearing a song playing that I didn't recognize. I muttered, "This song isn't on the playlist" and made Brandon go start it over. A few contractions later I asked "Where's the music?" because the room was silent. His phone had died. (Apparently the music was the only thing distracting me.)

I was so tired.

After a few more contractions (and screams), my doula said in my ear, "You're expending a lot of energy out the top end. See if you can channel it down. It's time to get this baby out." I heard her loud and clear.

I remember replying, "Yes. Okay. I can do this."

**8:27 a.m. Thursday, March 17.**

I'll never forget the ring of fire.

I could feel her head stretching to its widest point, and I heard Brandon saying, "Her head is almost out, babe, you can do it."

I felt the pain lessen, and I knew her head had come out. Completely exhausted, refusing to go through another contraction, and knowing the hardest part was over, I geared up and pushed with everything I had.

Everything moved quickly after that.

Our baby came into the world screaming. In the video, you can see the OB unwrap the umbilical cord from around her neck and hand her up through my legs and into my arms, but I had absolutely no idea about that at the time.

Everyone helped me lie down and skin-to-skin snuggle with her. I was in an exhausted state of shock.

*Sweet Sonora was born.*

**Some time after that, Thursday, March 17.**

As we were trying to get the baby to nurse, the OB said, "How would you like to no longer be pregnant?" She was referring to my placenta, which hadn't come out on its own yet.

They'd tried everything: fundal massage (which is NOT a massage), peeing, pushing, and nursing. It wasn't coming out. We were coming up on an hour, and they were starting to get a little more insistent on getting it out so they could prevent bleeding and cut the cord.

Finally, after some miserable pushing (which I'd thought I was done doing), fundal abuse, and Sonora latching, my placenta came out, and labor was over.

Brandon and I lay there with her: exhausted, starving, and in awe. After having my first-degree tear sutured, we Face-Timed our family and friends, had our stats monitored, and took a little nap. Then the birth center made us a gluten-free berry crisp, sang happy birthday to me, and we were all home and resting by 3 p.m.

Brandon says he can only describe Sonora's birth with one word: *Savage*.

And he's totally right.

In the most intense moments, I remember briefly wishing I had gone somewhere that administered pain medication, but looking back, I wouldn't have had it any other way.

Sonora's pregnancy and birth were the absolute most difficult physical and spiritual experiences I had ever been through.

And yet, the most rewarding.

When I look back on this experience, I'm grateful for all of the times I chose to do what was right for me—even if people didn't understand, or it seemed like I was choosing the difficult path instead of the obviously easier one.

There's something to be said about believing and proving to yourself that you can do hard things. Like, it was hard, and now it's not. *I fucking did it.*

*You can fucking do it.*

Easy peasy, piece of cake.

Remember: in life (and in business), everything you've ever done was once something you'd never done.

There was a time you didn't know how to ride a bike, and it was fucking scary.

There was a time you didn't know how to swim, and it was fucking scary.

There was a time you didn't know how to use a bidet and maybe you still don't because the idea of water shooting you in the butthole and missing and hitting you in the vagina instead sounds like a weird nightmare.

No matter what you're going through—no matter your current challenge—*you can fucking do it.*

You can do hard things.

Think of the you on the other side.

Stronger.

Braver.

More experienced.

Proud.

Accomplished AF.

All because you gave yourself a little vote of confidence and went after what you wanted.

My art director used to say, "If you possess the desire, you possess the qualities." And *fuck* if that isn't true.

You can write a book. *(If I can do it, so can you.)*

You can have your own cooking show.

You can get that promotion.

You can be a lettering artist.

If you feel pulled to do something: you were meant to do it. No matter how daunting or difficult it may seem in the beginning.

I know what you're doing right now. You're thinking, "Who am I to _____?" *(Insert wildest dream here.)*

Well, friend, who are you not to?

I was the same way with this book.

Who was I to write a book?

What did I have to say that was of value to anyone AND that hadn't been said already?

Who fucking cares?

And you know what? I fucking care.

At the very least, this book is one giant *Feel It to Heal It* release for me, and at the very most, you're finding yourself connecting with my stories and feeling inspired and motivated to heal, discover who you truly are, and step into your Main Character Energy.

*If you are connecting with my stories, and you have sixty seconds, would you take a moment to leave a review on my book on Amazon? It would truly mean the world to hear from you. And by leaving a review, you're helping to get this book into the hands of someone who really needs it right now. If you've already done it, ILYSM.*

I'd like to invite you now, to take a moment and reflect on all of the hard things you've done in your life. What are some of the mountains you've scaled? What are you fucking proud of?

Write TEN of them down—big or small, doesn't matter. Write down ten difficult things you've ever encountered and conquered in your life. Or more.

Seriously, stop reading and do it.
I'll wait.

Got 'em? *Good.*

You're going to need them in the next chapter.

## You Can Do Hard Things Affirmation

*I have everything I need to get through this.*

## You Can Do Hard Things Exercise

Write down ten difficult things you've ever encountered and conquered in your life.

# CELEBRATE ALL OF IT

Here are the ten things that came up for me when I did that exercise.

*Ten things that I'm celebrating the shit out of:*

1.  My traveling softball team in high school won the state championship. It was the first time I'd ever cried from joy. *Also maybe from heat stroke; we'll never truly know.*

2.  I was published twice in *Chicken Soup for the Soul* with a piece I wrote in college composition class about my dad.

3.  I survived multiple suicide attempts and a stay at a mental health facility.

4.  I was named a Top 10 Inspirational Self–Love and Confidence Coach to Follow in 2021 by Disrupt Magazine and Top Female Business Coach in 2023 by CoachFoundation.

5.  I've completed certifications as a Reiki Level II Energy Healer, Quantum Life and Success Coach, Emotional Freedom Technique (EFT/Tapping) Practitioner, TIME Techniques Practitioner, as well as a

Clinical Hypnotherapist, and Neuro Linguistic Programming (NLP) Practitioner.

6. In 2021, I graduated from a six-week stand-up comedy class. When our showcase was canceled, I decided to host my own virtual stand-up comedy show. With an incredible Zoom audience and thirty minutes of laughs, we raised more than $1200 for charity. It was such a success, I did it again in 2022 and 2023.

7. After a three-year journey *(more on this later)* I finally won the rights to trademark my signature coaching framework: Creating Confidence®!

8. I launched a membership program called The Creating Confidence® Society—where people can come together in a safe space and learn about themselves, build self-love, heal, grow, and connect—so I can help those unable to make the financial investment in 1:1 coaching gain the confidence to go after what they truly want in life and business. *Visit heymeganreed.com/society to join us.*

9. I grew and birthed a real-life baby. *People who give birth to a human being are seriously next-level magical creatures.*

10. I'm writing a damn BOOK! *(And shit, because you're reading this right now, I PUBLISHED a damn book!)*

So what was on your list?
*Ope, I'm gonna stop you right there.*
You were just comparing your story to mine, weren't you? And it stole your joy, didn't it?

Comparison is the thief of joy, my friend, but you already knew that, didn't you?

*Let me gently remind you that you are living in a completely different movie than I am.*

Think of how many awesome movies there are out there, and how each plot line is expertly crafted around the main character. *(Okay, most of them. Let's pretend shitty movies don't exist for a second here.)* If every movie had the same plot and high and low points, life would be pretty fucking boring, wouldn't it?

If you find yourself possessing the desire to achieve some of the same things on my list, then *congratulations!* You possess the qualities, and you've just identified something to add to your list of really cool dreams you're going after. *\*insert sunglasses emoji here\**

Let me tell you a little secret about celebrating.

When you make a conscious effort to celebrate every single win, no matter how big or small, you are choosing to vibrate higher. And people who vibrate higher tend to feel better and have more energy to work towards their big goals.

It's an incredible positive cycle.

So the next time a paycheck or client payment hits your bank account, let out a big-bellied *"WOO!"* and thank the Universe for the abundance.

Or the next time you win an award, land a promotion, or cross something off your bucket list, raise a glass to your efforts over a fancy sushi dinner.

Celebrations don't have to be huge or groundbreaking, either. Next time you get out of bed when you really didn't want to, give yourself a little hug and thank yourself for choosing to do another day.

Celebrating is an energetic practice of gratitude that returns back to us ten-fold. When you live in a state of gratitude, you're showing the Universe that you recognize and appreciate everything you have. You're affirming to the Universe: *Yes, this, and more please.*

When we can celebrate everything that we have while we have it, we are opening up the possibilities for even more.

A celebratory practice that Brandon and I like to do before bed every night *(okay, sometimes we fall off the wagon and don't do it for weeks at a time)*, is this: Before you turn out the lights, say three things out loud that you're grateful for from that day.

Sometimes the things are small, like, *"I'm grateful for tacos,"* or *"I'm grateful the day is over,"* and other times they're much bigger, like *"I'm grateful for my new client who just booked a $10k coaching package."*

Doing this before bed energetically shifts you into a state of gratitude, and when you're sleeping, your subconscious mind is hard at work programming all of this into long-term existence. (And if you don't have someone to say these out loud to, you can totally say them out loud to yourself/ the Universe/a pet, or grab a journal and write them down.)

The key is to celebrate.
Everything.
All of the time.
And have fun with it.

What's the point of crushing your dreams if all you ever do is forge onward to the next thing? Give yourself a moment to really *soak it all in.*

*When you get to the top of your mountain, turn around and take a look at the view.*

Release the idea that you must continue to climb in order to be successful—and accept the fact that you are successful and deserve to be celebrated, right where you are.

## Celebrate All of It Affirmation

*I'm proud of myself and everything I am accomplishing.*

## Celebrate All of It Exercise

Actually celebrate. Show someone your list. Have a little dance party. *CHEERS!*

# TRUST YOUR INTUITION

That little voice in your head?
Trust it.

And I don't mean the negative one—your ego—that's always up in your face and your business trying to keep you "safe" from falling off a stage, launching a business that fails, having a bad hair day on IG, or embarrassingly peeing your pants in front of the whole world.

I mean the little voice in your head that just *knows* stuff.

That feeling in your heart, that calling, the lil' nudge... that's your intuition. And it knows so much.

But if you're not listening, you could miss it completely.

I remember the day I found out I was supposed to give up gluten and dairy. It was nearly a year into my Crohn's Disease diagnosis, and I was tired of the steroids, immunosuppressants, procedures, and never-ending diarrhea. Nothing felt like it was working, I couldn't keep any weight on, and I was mentally exhausted from feeling like shit. *(Not to mention, I was depressed AF.)*

My dad (who also has Crohn's), had been in and out of the hospital with various Crohn's-related complications, including bowel obstructions and surgeries, and if I didn't do something else I was headed down the same road.

It was time to try something different.

*I just knew it.*

To make this long story much shorter, I saw a functional medicine internist and we ran blood work, food sensitivity panels, stool samples, and genetic testing. The results were overwhelming, and the consensus was this: I needed to lower the inflammation in my body, and the first step was a dietary change.

I had a whole list of foods flagged with inflammatory markers for me, and the biggest were gluten and dairy. Also on the list were things like eggs, black pepper, lemons, blueberries, bananas, and lima beans—and because I had a gene mutation that didn't allow me to process heavy metals, it was suggested I also consider eating organic.

I was overwhelmed when she went through the list, and I remember thinking, "Well, what the fuck CAN I eat?" The mere thought of giving up my mom's mac and cheese, chips and queso, pizza on my grandma's birthday, and fried chicken sandwiches had me spiraling.

But I was determined to feel better, tired of being let down by modern medicine, and ready to take responsibility for my own health. So, as an Enneagram One *(hello, rule follower)* with discipline as one of my strengths, I went home that day and threw away every single item in the fridge and pantry that I wasn't "supposed" to have.

It's weird looking back on it, but I just had this inner knowing that this was what I was supposed to be doing.

*Intuition.*

After a few months of being diligent with my recommended diet, I felt better and was ready to go off my Crohn's medication. I made an appointment with my gastroenterologist, told him I'd been focusing on my diet, lifestyle, and exercise and was feeling really good, and asked for his assistance weaning off my immunosuppressants and steroids.

He was mad.

His response was something along the lines of: *"You're going to be right back in here needing surgery. You'll have a colostomy bag by the time you're 30. This won't work. I can't help you."*

He made me feel like I was going to die if I went off my medication.

Well suck it, Dr. Not McHelpful. I'm fucking thriving.

If I had listened to him—had I not trusted my intuition that day—I very well could be in the same position my dad is today. Surgery scars, yearly ER visits, and medicine trials.

Thanks, intuition.

Another example of a time where trusting my intuition was a big fucking risk but it paid off was when I began the trademarking process of Creating Confidence®.

*See that little trademark R thingie there next to it?*

When I hired a legal team to trademark my signature coaching framework, they did their initial research and came back to me with a "tornado warning," essentially recommending I change the name because there was already something similar out there and the odds of my trademark going through successfully were extremely low, so it wouldn't be a wise use of my investment to go through with it.

I was devastated.

I *knew* THIS was what my program was supposed to be called.

Creating Confidence®, damnit. I was emotionally attached.

I told them I was going to do some market research and would get back to them on a different name. *I did not actually do any market research. Instead, I just ignored the problem.*

Months later, after my final payment went through and I had paid for the trademark I wasn't even actively pursuing at the time, I reached out, asked some clarifying questions, provided examples for why I believed I could win the trademark, and told them to run it anyways.

My intuition straight-up said *watch me win this.*

And here we are, YEARS later, and I won the trademark.

*Creating Confidence® is mine!*

All because I trusted my intuition.

Real Main Character Energy vibes, amirite?

That's what trusting your intuition is all about.

Going after whatever it is that you want, regardless of what anyone else is saying, because *you know in your soul that's what is meant for you.*

That you've fucking GOT THIS.

"Don't put your picture on the cover of your book," a book coach advised, unless I was a celebrity or recognizable public figure.

*Watch me,* I thought.

"You can't sell confidence," a man said on a podcast I was listening to about nailing your marketing and messaging so you can make millions.

*Watch me,* I thought.

"Don't feed your baby to sleep," the Internet says, warning you'll create a devastating sleep association with milk and make bedtime routines difficult in the future.

*I'm gonna do it because that's what feels right.*

I've run into this a ton as a new mom, actually.

The differing opinions on bed sharing and sleep training and wake windows and feeding schedules and what worked for your mother-in-law. It's truly fucking exhausting trying to decide which information is for you and which isn't.

Lemme tell you this—whether you have children or not—you know, more than anyone else in the world, what is right for you.

Your intuition is there for a reason.

Listen to it.
Trust it.

## Trust Your Intuition Affirmation

*I am wise, intuitive, and connected to my inner guidance.*

## Trust Your Intuition Exercise

Set a five-minute timer, get comfortable, and meditate silently in your own way. Let your thoughts simply come and go as they may. Witness them, and release them. Ask for answers, ask for general guidance, ask for nothing, ask for whatever it is you need. Allow yourself to sink in, quiet the noise, and just listen. When you feel complete, you may want to write down what you received.

# YOU ARE THE EXPERT

"Who am I to do this?"
- *Literally every single client I've ever coached*

Bitch, who are you NOT to?

People are so often under the impression that to be seen as an expert, they have to know literally every single thing about a topic.

I used to believe that I would never be able to call myself a personal development, confidence, or boundaries expert because I wasn't Brené Brown, Nedra Tawaab, or Tony Robbins. If you're not the best in the field, you're not an expert... right?

Wrong.

You do NOT have to know everything to be an expert. You just have to know a little bit more than the people you are helping. If you've walked on a similar path and you're a step or ten ahead of them, great! If you have some tools that work, perfect. You don't have to be a master, and you don't have to have invented the wheel on this subject, either. You have your own take, your own angle, and your people will be attracted to what you offer.

You think I know everything about building a business, setting boundaries, and showing up with confidence and authenticity?

LOL. Absolutely not.

But what I *do* have is more knowledge than the people I'm guiding.

And as I continue to learn and level up, so do they.

We learn from each other, actually. If my students' learnings ever surpass mine, then I will feel proud knowing I have done my job well.

And it doesn't matter what your BFF Jill is over there doing. She's an expert, too, and that has nothing to do with whether or not you can also be an expert.

*We can all be experts.*

It's about having confidence in yourself, regardless of what someone else is doing. Because we often—if not *always*—overestimate others and underestimate ourselves. We think, "So-and-so knows so much more than me! They've got it all figured out," while at the same time, they're thinking the exact same thing about you.

Tell me, dear reader, when was the last time you gave yourself the benefit of the doubt?

What if you gave yourself the credit you give to everyone else? It'd feel fucking powerful, wouldn't it?

How would it feel to know you're the expert in your story?

There's no one on this entire planet who knows more about you than you do. No one has had the exact same experiences. Felt your feelings. Lived your life.

*And that makes you an expert.*

How does it feel when you read that?

Raise your hand if your inner critic said something like, "Yeah, sure, but... *insert dumbass reason your inner bullshitter told you that you're not an expert here.*

I'm not surprised, honestly. Imposter syndrome (that feeling where you're worried people will realize you're a fraud and you have absolutely no idea what you're doing and they'll call you out on it and you'll have to admit that you're zero percent qualified), is something I help my clients with. I see it all the time.

While it can be super easy to listen to that negative voice calling you a fraud, instead, I want you to simply recognize that it's popping up at all.

Oftentimes, "imposter syndrome" is just the label we choose for something that goes much, much deeper. It's the tip of a giant-ass iceberg that's barely visible above the water, ready to sink the Titanic (you). Let's take a look:

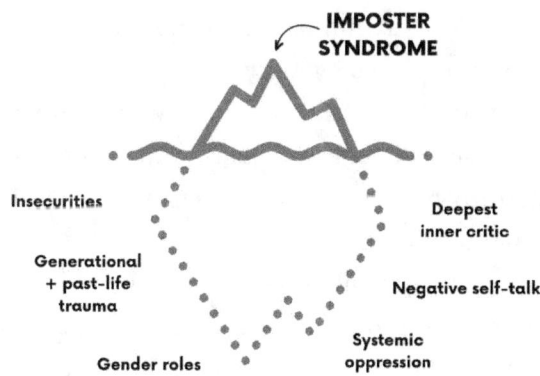

When I go deeper with my clients in coaching sessions, we often uncover that what they had self-diagnosed as imposter syndrome was actually a combination of many things, for example: negative self-talk, generational (ancestral) trauma, past-life trauma, gender roles, or systemic oppression.

And these things come up big for my clients any time they're doing something out of their comfort zone. Any time they're doing something against the grain or cultural norm.

Any time they're doing something brave.

Let's use another movie example. If you've never seen *The Devil Wears Prada,* 10 out of 10 recommend. (Also, where have you been?) Meryl Streep and Anne Hathaway have serious Main Character Energy vibes.

*The Devil Wears Prada* is a popular film that touches heavily on the theme of imposter syndrome. It follows the story of Andy Sachs (played by Anne Hathaway), a recent college graduate who lands a job as an assistant to the amazingly demanding and highly influential fashion magazine editor, Miranda Priestly (played by Meryl Streep).

Throughout the film, Andy struggles with feelings of inadequacy and self-doubt as she tries to fit into the glamorous and cutthroat world of fashion journalism. She initially feels like an outsider and an imposter among her fashionable and sophisticated colleagues.

However, as she grows more confident and assertive in her role, Andy begins to realize that her unique perspective and outsider status actually give her an edge and valuable perspective in her work. Through her experiences, she learns to trust her instincts, embrace her strengths, and overcome her feelings of imposter syndrome.

She keeps going, regardless of the fear.

Feelings of self-doubt are totally understandable.

Doing new things can be scary. Calling yourself an expert feels like next-level shit, but you are worthy of that title. You are worthy of that promotion. You are worthy of that raise. *You are worthy of it all.*

Because what's meant for you will not pass you, and it's time to step into your power and claim the badass main character that you are.

Next time you notice your self doubt creeping in, perhaps it's simply a sign to keep going.

*To stay the course.*
*To keep pushing the limits of what you're capable of.*
*To continue leaving your comfort zone.*

Keep going, my friend, because YOU are the expert.

*It's time to act like it.*

## You Are the Expert Affirmation

*I am the expert of my life.*

## You Are the Expert Exercise

Get out your journal and brain dump five things you're an expert on. *(What are five things you could give a 30-minute presentation on right now?)*

# STAND TRUE TO YOUR BELIEFS

I believe that washing your face is the biggest crock of shit I've ever heard. Tell me one person who, at the end of their life, said their biggest regret was not washing their face more.

I don't wash my face, and I have great fucking skin.

That's not entirely true. I wash my face when I shower. Which is as infrequent as possible because I hate the idea of it until I'm in there and then I live there for the unforesee-able future.

I also don't wear makeup that often.

Or sunscreen. *gasp*

Or deodorant, really. (Although this one is mostly because I forget.)

I believe the chemicals we're sold to put on our bodies and cleanse our skin and prevent wrinkles are the exact reasons we need said products.

I'm no scientist, but I know for a damn fact that the more you wash your hair, the more you have to wash your hair.

I'm not afraid of aging. I'm not afraid of wrinkles. I'm not afraid of my gray hair. (For now... ask me again in five years.)

What I am afraid of—or at least, deeply aware of—is society's persistent messaging that we're not good enough the way that we are and that we have to conform to a set of unrealistic/unattainable standards and make ourselves smaller/less weird to fit in.

The whole "keeping up with the Joneses" thing.

We believe we have to have the trendy things our influencer friends are always talking about on social media because if we don't, we are seen as somehow "less than" or "not enough." But literally who is anyone else to say that having a big house, a 14-step skincare routine, and a giant water cup makes you hot or not?

What if, instead of believing that you have to be the same as everyone else, you believed that you were perfect, just as you are?

It's time to challenge the things you feel like you "should" be doing. Shoulds are shit, remember? They're an unspoken obligatory pressure we put on ourselves.

Let's look at the movie *Brave.*

This entire movie centers around the theme of standing firm in your beliefs, releasing the "shoulds," and being true to who you are. It tells the story of Merida, a badass archer princess in the Scottish kingdom of DunBroch.

Merida outwardly defies traditional expectations and challenges the generational customs of her kingdom, particularly the practice of arranged marriages. She fights for her independence and the freedom to determine her own destiny. *Like I said, total badass.*

Throughout the movie, Merida remains steadfast in her beliefs and refuses to compromise her values, even in the face of adversity. *I won't give too much away, but accidentally turning her mom into a bear was a real mess for her.* Her journey showcases the importance of staying true to yourself and standing up for what you believe in, despite all of society's pressure.

*Brave* delivers a powerful message about individuality, self-discovery, and the courage to follow one's own path, inspiring viewers to embrace their unique identities and stand true to their Main Character Energy.

Your beliefs are what make you who you are.

*What make you unique.*

There is no one on this Earth who has every single, exact same belief about everything as you, and that's pretty magical isn't it?

Imagine if Bella Swan in the movie *Twilight* believed, like everyone else, that the Cullen family—full of beautiful vampires—was weird and stayed away from them.

What a boring fucking movie that would have been, right?

Imagine if Leonardo DiCaprio's character, Jack, in *Titanic*, believed—like everyone else on the ship—that Rose (Kate Winslet) was out of his league. He would have never rescued her from jumping off the back of the boat and sparked one of the greatest love stories of all time.

Imagine how different the movie *Zootopia* would be if the main character bunny, Judy Hops, believed she was just meant to be a farmer—like her family—for the rest of her life instead of what she truly dreamed of being: a police officer in the big city.

Your beliefs shape your world, your decisions, and your perspective.

*What do you believe?*

## Stand True to Your Beliefs Affirmation

*I stand firm in my beliefs, form my own opinions, and embrace my unique perspectives.*

## Stand True to Your Beliefs Exercise

What do you believe? Journal ten things you feel in your soul to be true for you. If you want, you can complete these sentences: "I believe in..." "I believe that..."

# KEEP IT REAL

Can we talk about the clusterfuck that is the female human experience?

You have a kid. (Or maybe you don't, but I do.)

And it's really tough and you can't go back and undo that and you're sleep deprived and your mental health is tanking and your marriage is suffering and you're a walking milk machine and you're really just not sure you ever want another one.

And then one random night your husband goes rogue on a potential ovulation day, according to your app that you're tracking your cycle in so you know when it's cool that you're acting a fool, and you immediately spiral.

You don't want to be pregnant.

You would literally be unwell if you were pregnant right now.

So you're peeing on pregnancy tests. Every morning, knowing damn well you're not due for your period for another ten days. But you do it anyway, because you need to know.

You're ANALYZING the spot where a little line would show up if you were pregnant, wondering if your eyes are playing tricks on you and if you see something there or if it's just your mind fucking around.

And as if you just couldn't wait ten days to find out if you get your period or not.

Because PMS and early pregnancy symptoms feel the same.

You're moody. Your boobs hurt. You've got cramps. You're tired as hell. The meal your husband made for dinner last night tasted like shit, and you ate an entire gluten-free cake leftover from your daughter's first birthday straight out of the freezer.

Everything is suspicious.

You're calculating mathematical equations in your head and drawing investigative suspect maps with pictures and string on the whiteboard in your office. Like:

*If I were to get pregnant, this baby would be born in fucking January, which is the worst month, and do I really want an Aquarius baby?*

*And is this weight I'm gaining from being pregnant, or is it time to stop inhaling funfetti cakes? Or are those even mutually exclusive?*

*And I was pregnant over the holidays last time and it fucking sucked and I swore I was NOT gonna do THAT again.*

*But if I WERE to be pregnant, I don't want that little egg inside me absorbing this bad energy and thinking it's not wanted, because that's a fucking thing, right?*

So you start working on getting on board with the idea that this might be happening.

Yeah, this is fine. God's plan, or whatever.

We can do this. It's meant to be. Our daughter's going to have a SIBLING!

So now, you're like, okay, cool, let's go.

Let's fucking do this.

We're hyped.

We GOT this.

And then you get your period.

And all of a sudden this balloon you've been blowing up, that you didn't even want to blow up, is deflated. So now you're mourning what you maybe didn't even want in the first place because you made yourself get cool with it just in case it happened and then it didn't, which is a relief but now you're wondering—wait, did I actually want to be pregnant, or am I sad because I made myself get okay with the idea because I thought it was gonna happen?

And now you're feeling selfish because of all the people out there who want to be pregnant but are struggling and here you are just peeing on sticks and praying you don't see an extra little blue line.

And the cycle continues every single month.

*And people wonder why we're moody.*

The duality of life is so real, isn't it?

I woke up thinking about this after sharing about my struggles with motherhood, pregnancy, and postpartum in one of my online comedy shows for charity.

That night I found myself having a vulnerability hangover, wondering, *"What if people think I don't love or deserve my baby because I'm not 100% thriving and talking about how magical it is to be a mom every fucking minute?"*

The amount of DMs I got thanking me for being so open and raw and talking about the real struggles was off the charts. And it got me thinking.

*Why don't we talk about the hard shit?*

Because somewhere along the way, we bought into the story that people only want to see the highlights of our lives. We bought into the idea that we aren't allowed to struggle or be honest or share anything less than sunshine and rainbows and good vibes only.

But here's the reality: *Two things can be true at once.*

It's not this OR that, it's this AND that.

- You can love your newborn baby AND miss your old life.
- You can value a relationship AND set a boundary.
- You can feel some type of way about your postpartum body AND grateful for all the miracles it has provided.

- You can be terrified of public speaking AND deliver a bomb-ass presentation.
- You can find social media daunting AND show up daily with fire content.
- You can be depressed AND experience moments of joy.

Just because you feel one way about something doesn't mean you can't feel another way about it, too.

**Fuck the highlight reel.**
**Share it all.**

When you do, you give others around you permission to feel their feelings and let go of the comparison trap, too, so if they're not feeling spunky and sparkly all the time that's totally normal and they're not alone.

Because contrary to what we see on social media, emotions are not mutually exclusive or singular. They are all-encompassing.

*Feel it all. Embrace it all. Honor it all.*

Now, don't get me wrong. I'm not saying you should hop on a live video every single day and tell the entire world how everything in your life sucks.

You know that wouldn't serve anyone, and it especially wouldn't serve you.

What I'm saying is that it's okay for you to be a human.

It's okay to admit when you need help—or share how you got help.

My rule of thumb for keeping it real: When I'm in the shit, I'm in it.

I don't generally share much about what I'm going through at the moment so I can process and work through my thoughts and feelings first, on my own terms. I don't cryptically post a quote on Facebook about trusting in the Lord and asking for prayers.

*Sorry if you've ever done that LOL.*

I allow myself the space and grace to grow through what I'm going through—and then when—and IF—it feels right, I share. Usually in the form of an email, blog post, or Instagram caption, complete with the lessons and learnings and what I did to work through it. So if by chance there's someone in the world dealing with that same thing, maybe my story will help them.

I'm here to normalize the human experience, you know?

To remind you that the main characters do indeed go through some shit.

Can you imagine a movie where there was no conflict or resolution? All highs and wins?

Me either.

So tell me, where in your life have you been hiding behind a mask of sunshine and rainbows, and how can you let go of the pressure to have it all together?

It's time to keep it real, my friend.

## Keep It Real Affirmation

*I release the pressure I've put on myself to have it all together, all the time.*

## Keep It Real Exercise

Journal: Where in your life have you been hiding behind a mask, and how can you let go of that pressure to have it all together?

# HOLD THE VISION

There's going to come a time when you'll wonder what the fuck you're even doing.

What was it all for?

What's the fucking point?

Who even gives a royal shit?

And you're going to want to give up.

To turn around and go back down the mountain.

To say, "This is too hard," and decide to call it quits.

I know, because I've been there.

I've been in a place that felt like rock bottom, where it felt like there was no light at the end of the tunnel. It was right after Sonora was born, and it truly felt like the blows just kept coming.

For starters, we had a newborn baby who was always crying, and we had no idea why. As it turned out, she had tongue and lip ties that weren't allowing her to latch correctly and transfer much milk from me. I sat there and ugly cried while she chomped at my bloody nipples for the first week straight, exhausted from no sleep, and physically feeling like I got hit by a bus.

Oh, and I prolapsed again, so I was supposed to be spending my time horizontal to try and retrain my uterus that it lives inside, and not out.

Brandon and I took turns having mental breakdowns. If one of us was crying, the other was consoling both the baby and a grown adult. For the first three months of her life, we were completely under water—and little did we know at the time, it was only going to get worse.

Three weeks before going into labor, I had closed up shop with my coaching clients—*because we thought I was going to deliver early, remember?* My business was running on what little reserves it had so I wasn't able to pay myself, but Brandon's chiropractic patients had been slowly picking up, and I was excited to pass the financial torch to him and take a break from business-ing for a couple months and focus on mom-ing.

It happened in slow motion, yet somehow all of a sudden and all at once.

The bills started coming in, and the income didn't.

We'd maxed out one of our credit cards buying groceries, we were three months behind on rent, and there was $0 in our bank account. I kept getting email after email about rejected payments and overdraft fees.

I took out a loan in my business to pay for shit.

The stack of bills just kept growing, and I stopped opening them. I quit answering the phone, too. Because it was always someone reminding me about a bill that I couldn't pay.

Our marriage was in shambles.

We were power struggling who got to work when, and who was watching Sonora—hello, it was always me—and the fact that he got to leave the house and go to the office and treat a couple patients and hang out with his gym friends and pretend he didn't have a family and a baby and a dog and a mess at home made me so resentful. I was envious.

Envious that his body looked the same as it did a year ago: no stretch marks or squishy skin, his hormones weren't shifting wildly, he wasn't leaking milk, his cervix wasn't hanging out of him, and he was just, overall, physically fine.

Not to mention I had postpartum depression, and I thought about killing myself every single day.

Then my cat died.

Bellatrix (Bella, for short) had kidney failure and early signs of cancer. Midnight at the emergency vet, and we had the option to Hail Mary a dialysis treatment and blood transfusion so *maybe* she would be comfortable for a little longer—but we were already drowning in debt—and to put her down, we had to max out another one of our credit cards.

*I'm literally crying as I write this knowing I couldn't afford to give her every last effort available.*

She hadn't eaten or kept anything down in weeks, so when she scarfed her last meal of tuna and collapsed in my arms when they injected her little black paw with whatever the fuck it is they use to put pets to sleep, I was beside myself.

I felt guilty for not bringing her to the vet sooner, and I was heartbroken to lose the first pet I had ever rescued.

*I thought she was going to live forever.*

I don't know that I've ever cried as hard as I did for her—not even when my grandparents died. Losing a pet, no matter the circumstances, is a pain unimaginable.

On the night we knew it was absolutely past time to take Bella to the vet, Brandon and I took a video of us ugly crying in my office and talking about everything going on in our lives at that moment. Our newborn was sleeping in the room next door.

*"This is going to be the story we tell on stage some day to massive crowds of people who want to hear from us,"* we said.

And now here I am, telling you this story in my book.

As a reminder that you must hold the vision.

You must keep the faith, remember your why, and hold on to hope.

Even when things are tough.

Actually, *especially when things are tough.*

Because you are here for a reason.

If and when you come upon a time in your life where you feel like completely giving up on your dreams, know this: I hear you, and I see you.

You will get through this.

When you zoom out completely and look over your entire timeline, this difficult time is nothing more than a bump in the road that taught you some really important lessons on your personal journey.

This is the part of the movie where the main character hits a turning point and decides to do something different. It's the final conflict before resolution and smooth sailing.

You could 100% give up. But that's not the kind of person you are, is it? You've never been the type of person to fight hard for something and then roll over when things get tough.

So keep going, my friend.
Even if it feels like the Universe is raining a disastrous shit storm down on you.

Hold the vision.
*You've got this.*

## Hold the Vision Affirmation

*I can do hard things.*

## Hold the Vision Exercise

Reflect: What is your vision? What are you doing it all for?

# TRUST THE TIMING OF YOUR LIFE

People always ask me at networking events, "So, how did you get into coaching?"

And I should totally have a romantic answer for it by now that isn't, "Oh, you know, I just sort of fell into it," because their eyes immediately gloss over and look around the room for their next person to talk to.

I do have a better answer to this question, actually. It's just a web of realizations and feelings and callings and lessons that I have yet to figure out how to convey in a paragraph succinct enough to shout in a loud and crowded bar full of businesspeople making connections.

I remember two things that were the matches that started the burning flame which became my coaching business.

The first one was a video call I was on with my younger sister in 2019. She had recently left her job and was trying to figure out what was next for her. We were updating her resume and practicing interview questions and answers.

Now, this was before I had any kind of coaching certifications or really even any knowledge about what a coach was or did, but I was taking her pretty deep in an effort to help her see the skills she had to offer and that she could do whatever she wanted and be successful at it. *(You know, because that's what sisters do, right?)*

I don't remember the exact question I asked her, but I do remember the way she looked at me, started to cry, and told me she didn't know who she was.

I felt my heart break for her and knew in my soul that I could help her and anyone else going through something similar.

The second one was an incredible opportunity that I said yes to even though I was nervous as shit.

My biz bestie, Taylor, had an extra ticket to Brendon Burchard's 2019 Influencer Summit in San Diego and a free place to stay. All I had to do was catch a flight.

Now, this was in the early days of our friendship, and I still had a lot of money mindset work to do. I'd never traveled with Taylor, I'd never been to a personal development conference, and I'd never just spent $500 to last-minute hop on a plane.

But I knew this was a sign from the Universe.

The summit was incredible, the California food was amazing, and I left feeling fired up as shit about creating an impact in the world—grateful I felt the fear and said YES anyway.

*Me at Influencer Summit 2019*

I've learned so many lessons over the years.
About life.
About myself.
About taking risks.
About writing a book.
About running a business.

*But I wouldn't have been ready for them any sooner.*
These lessons came to me exactly when I needed them.

I have so many lessons I want to leave you with, but I know that they won't all land for you right now. *That's why you should read this book again and again. Read it every year. Pick it up and flip to a random page and read it, because I promise you, something new will resonate that didn't even make you blink the first time.*

If I can leave you with anything at all, I want to leave you knowing that everything you need will come to you exactly when you need it, and not a moment sooner.

Trust the timing of your life, knowing that you are exactly where you're supposed to be right now. You're not behind. You are on your own timeline, and worrying about said timeline is a choice. With most things in life, it's super easy to get stuck worrying about shit. Playing the "what-if" game, ya know?

You can worry all day long, giving yourself unnecessary stress, or you can lean into faith and trust in The Universe, knowing the outcome will be the same whether you worry or not... so what's the purpose of worrying?

Focus on the present moment and lean into the trust that everything is happening exactly as it should, exactly *when* it should.

You, my friend, are exactly where you're supposed to be.

## Trust the Timing of Your Life Affirmation

*I trust the timing of my life. Everything I need comes to me exactly when I need it.*

## Trust the Timing of Your Life Exercise

Reflect: How can you lean into the knowing that you are exactly where you're supposed to be right now?

# YOU ARE THE MAIN CHARACTER

I'm sorry, the old *insert your name* isn't here right now. Why? 'Cuz she's dead.

It's time we lay to rest (in peace, of course), the person you used to be. The old you before you read this book. The non-player character who:

- Said yes to literally everything because you felt obligated to make others happy

- Used to stay silent when things bothered you or hurt your feelings

- Procrastinated on your dreams because you were afraid of failing

- Looked at yourself in the mirror and feel disappointed

- Felt like you weren't good enough, smart enough, beautiful enough, strong enough

- Felt like a fraud in everything you did

- Let perfectionism and people-pleasing rule your life

- Worked nonstop until you burnt out... every single year

- Held grudges and harbored resentment like it was your job

- Hid your true self out of fear of rejection
- Thought people were constantly judging you and your actions.

It's time to let all that go, to not give a single flying fuck—in the absolute best way possible—and embrace your Main Character Energy.

You! Magical, fucking incredible and brilliant YOU, the main character, who:

- Says no to things that don't energetically align
- Knows you are worthy and enough, just as you are
- Ditched your self-doubt
- Rests when you need to
- Let go of the incessant need to be perfect
- Loves the person you see in the mirror (*and damn, do they look good these days!*)
- Goes after what you want, even if you're afraid
- Makes a conscious effort to forgive yourself and others
- Shows all the way up as YOU (and you fucking love that person).

Aren't you ready to let go of the version of you that's no longer serving you?

Aren't you ready to love who you truly are and discover the magic that's already within you?

(I know I was.)

It's time to stop hiding, my dear main character.

There's a scene in the movie *The Holiday*, where one of the main characters, Iris Simpkins (played by Kate Winslet) has an empowering realization about her own worth and the importance of embracing her role as the protagonist in her own story. *(10/10 recommend this movie.)*

In this scene, Iris is having a heartfelt conversation with her elderly neighbor. Iris was obsessed with a guy who didn't give a shit about her and was feeling disappointed and invisible. Her neighbor, with his wisdom and life experience as a screenwriter, hits her with a unique perspective shift.

He says to her, "Iris, in the movies, we have leading ladies, and we have the best friend. You, I can tell, are a leading lady. But for some reason, you're behaving like the best friend."

*insert mic drop emoji here* (*Is there a mic drop emoji? Why the fuck not?*)

He encourages her to step into her own power and embrace her role as the main character. This scene serves as a turning point for Iris, as she begins to recognize her own self-worth and begins to take charge of her life. It inspires her to make bold choices and seek out her own happiness, rather than being a supporting player in someone else's narrative.

This book, I hope, is a turning point for you.
*The permission you've been searching for.*

People always ask me, "Where do you get the courage to post/share/write about your life?"

And sometimes I'm speechless.

"I don't know," I say. "I just don't second-guess myself."

And I think that's the key.

I don't second-guess myself.

I know who I am.

I'm not afraid of being human.

I've embraced my Main Character Energy.

And now, I'm passing the torch to you.

Go put in the work.

Get to know yourself.

Own your weird.

Establish badass boundaries.

Set goals. *And crush them.*

Allow yourself to dream big.

Give yourself grace.

Keep it real.

Leave perfectionism in the dust.

Stand true to your beliefs.

Trust your intuition.

Celebrate all of it.

Let shit go. *Like, really do it.*

Seek internal validation.

Leave your comfort zone. *Consistently.*

Get out of your own damn way.

Hold the vision, even when things are tough.

Hire coaches *(ahem, heyoooo)* to help you with the areas you want to improve.

Release old stories.
Step into your favorite version of yourself.
100% go after what you want.

Because once you begin to love and trust yourself as who you truly are, you start showing up differently.

You stand up for what you believe in.
You feel courageous.
You feel confident.
You feel authentically yourself.

*It's time, isn't it?*

Time to quit waiting to be who you already are.
You are worthy.
You are beautiful.
You are loved.
You are enough.
You are powerful.
You are badass.
NOW.

*And you know it, don't you?*

You are the main character of your life, so why act like a supporting role?

When you look back on your life, you'll want to be proud of yourself, won't you?
For the choices you made.

For the risks you took.
For the things you accomplished.

Or maybe you'll wish you'd done things differently.
Trusted your intuition.
Gone on that trip.
Said yes to yourself.

When you look back on your life, you want to know you did everything you could to show up as your most true and authentic self while following your dreams, don't you?

*I know I do.*

So go after what you want.
Write the book.
Plan the trip.
Share your expertise.
Make an impact.
Get the tattoo.

It's YOUR TURN.
To fully live your life.
To take the leap.
To go after your dreams.
To set boundaries.
To start your business.
To ditch the need to people please.
To hit that next income goal.
To quit your soul-sucking job.
To raise your prices.

To speak on that stage.

To tell your story.

To fucking do the damn thing.

It's YOUR TURN to be unapologetic about your passions and the things that light you up.

Because time is finite.

It is your most precious resource.

And you're done wasting it.

You're done putting your dreams off "for another time," or "when the kids are older," or "when things slow down a bit."

*You're SO FUCKING DONE dimming your light to make others comfortable.*

It's time to be unapologetically yourself.

Being the main character of your own story is a powerful concept.

It means taking ownership of your life and living on your own terms. It's a journey of self-discovery and personal growth, where you'll learn to embrace your strengths and weaknesses, and use them to create a life that is truly meaningful and fulfilling for you.

It also means being resilient and overcoming challenges and obstacles. Every great story has its ups and downs, but this is where you harness the strength and determination to overcome them because you're in control of your own destiny and have the power to shape your future in any way you choose.

By stepping into—and shining with—your Main Character Energy, you can create a life full of purpose, passion, and joy because you're showing up with authenticity and confidence.

You're showing up as YOU.

You—the writer, director, and star of your own journey—and only you, have the power to create the story you want to live.

It's time to embrace your role as the main character and make your life a movie worth watching at the end of it.

*The possibilities for you are endless.*

# ACKNOWLEDGMENTS

Thank you, Universe, for the intuitive download to write a book and call it *Main Character Energy.* Thank you for the energy and capacity to complete it, even when I felt like I never would. I'm so grateful to you! And I want to acknowledge these people as well:

**Brandon**—Thank you for the grounded love, the delicious food, and the caffeine. I'm grateful to have you as my life partner, and I know Sonora loved her weekends with Dad while I was away furiously writing this book. You're the best around.

**Mom and Dad**—Thank you for your love and support... Through all of it. Your faith, trust, and belief in me have never faltered, even though most days you still have no idea what it is I do in my coaching business LOL.

**Emily**—Thank you for always checking on your little sister. I'm so grateful to have you as a sounding board for all of my questions, whether about diaper changes, marriage, or nap times.

**Laura**—Thank you for being the inspiration for my calling. I'll always have your back, anytime you need me.

**Kelsey**—Thanks for seeing me, and for hanging in there through the cover-design process and never-ending requests for feedback. Oh, and thanks for making me buy that sparkly dress for the cover, too. It was truly a vibe.

**Emily**—To the original roommate who truly let me fly my weird flag, thank you. It meant (and still means) a lot to feel safe to be my true self around you.

**Taylor**—There's no way this book (or my coaching business) would be here right now if it weren't for you, our endless messages back and forth, and our weekend getaway writing retreats. Thanks for keeping me from burning it all down and helping me light it all up instead.

**Jill**—I seriously could not have done this without your expertise, words of confidence, and moral support through the entire writing and editing process. Thank you for the countless reminders and permission I needed to stay true to my authentic voice.

**Alex**—You taught me how to stand up for myself, how to laugh at myself, and how to embrace my Main Character Energy. Thank you for your pivotal presence in my life.

**Sage**—I'm so glad the Universe sent you to edit this book. Your expert insight, thoughtful comments, and positive feedback gave me life.

**To the teachers who saw me**—Mrs. Koerner, Mrs. Livingston, Mr. Weller, Mrs. Divel, Mrs. Erickson, Mrs. Poland, and so many more. Thank you for embracing my weird, acknowledging my journey, and encouraging me to express myself. I am so grateful for you and the impact you had on my life. The world needs more leaders like you.

**To my peer reviewers**—You really did the most. Thank you for devoting your time and energy to the success of this book. Espresso martinis for all of you.

**To my launch team**—Your positive hype and feedback kept me going more than you could ever know. Thank you for sharing MCE with the world. You're the real MVPs.

**To my clients, students, and Society members**—I love you so fucking much, and I'm honored to be part of your story. Thank you for inspiring content inside these chapters. YOU are the magical main characters.

**To Holton, Kansas**—Thanks for the hospitality, the boxed wine, the gluten-free pizza, and the coffee. You're cute.

**To you**—Thank you for coming along this journey with me. It means the world to have played even a minuscule part in your story. Keep going, okay?

**To anyone I forgot**—I'm probably lying awake thinking about it. *Thanks a lot.*

# RESOURCES

## Confidence Blindspot Quiz

A fun, *free*, and intuitive eight-question online quiz designed to help you uncover where you've been secretly holding yourself back—as told by your favorite pop-culture television characters:

https://heymeganreed.com/quiz

## Creating Confidence® Society

The personal development community with everything you need to step into your Main Character Energy: support, accountability, education, strategy, coaching, community, and tough love. Join us inside the Society for monthly masterclasses and workshops on hot topics, guest expert trainings, live group coaching calls, quarterly challenges, deep relationship building, and subconscious healing:

https://heymeganreed.com/society

## Creating Confidence® Course

Self-discovery, self-mastery, and self-expression team up inside eight video modules designed to help you discover the magic of who you truly are so you can be unapologetically and creatively yourself. The only course on confidence you'll ever need. Workbooks, affirmations, and bonuses included. You receive all content and future updates, for life:

https://heymeganreed.com/creating-confidence

## Badass Boundaries Blueprint

Stop saying yes when you want to say no. Learn how to protect your peace, ditch your inner people pleaser, and communicate badass boundaries inside nine video modules. Workbooks, affirmations, and bonus Emotional Freedom Technique (EFT/Tapping) For Better Boundaries healing exercise included. You receive all content and future updates, for life:

https://heymeganreed.com/bbb

## Quantum Coaching Academy

Turn your coaching calling into a coaching craft and become a world-class certified quantum coach. The Quantum Coaching Academy is a six-month certification program for those who are ready to step into world-class coaching & leadership. It is internationally accredited through the International Coaching Federation (ICF) and designed to make you the most confident coach in the room by giving you a proven methodology that works:

https://heymeganreed.com/qca

# ABOUT THE AUTHOR

**MEGAN REED** is an award-winning Confidence Coach, Best-Selling Author, Speaker, and Reiki Energy Healer from Chapman, Kansas—here to help you own your weird and unleash your *Main Character Energy*. She's the founder of the Creating Confidence® Society and mastermind behind the Badass Boundaries Blueprint—on a mission to help you discover the magic of who you truly are so you can ditch your inner critic, get out of your own way, and unapologetically achieve your wildest dreams.

As a Certified Quantum Life and Success Coach, Reiki Healer, NeuroLinguistic Programming (NLP) Practitioner, Clinical Hypnotherapist, Business Coach, Emotional Freedom Technique (EFT) Practitioner, Boundaries Expert, Manifestation Mastermind and Self-Proclaimed Badass, Megan takes a heart-centered approach to helping her clients heal and release what's holding them back, overcome imposter syndrome, and let go of people pleasing so they can embody their most confident self. *The one who goes after everything they ever wanted.*

She's the sarcastic, spiritual, Frankie-to-your-Grace, no-bullshit, self-love cheerleader you've been looking for.

# A NOTE FROM MEGAN

*Hey friend! If you loved this book, please consider leaving a five-star Amazon review (you're the greatest!) or buying a copy for someone you care about. And please keep in touch on social, I'd love to hear from you—DM me your biggest takeaway, won't you?! It's been an absolute honor having you on this journey.*
*XOXO, Megan*

# CONNECT WITH ME ON SOCIAL
## @HEYMEGANREED

For speaking inquiries + to join my email list, please head to: HEYMEGANREED.COM